DISCOVERING BIBLICAL TREASURES

UNDERSTANDING MICAH

A COMMENTARY ON THE BOOK OF MICAH USING ANCIENT BIBLE STUDY METHODS - UPDATED

Michael Harvey Koplitz

This edition 2024 copyright © by Michael Harvey Koplitz

All rights reserved. No part of this publication may be reproduced or transmitted in any form or by any means without permission of the publisher.

All Scripture quotations, unless otherwise noted, are taken from the *New American Standard Bible®*, Copyright © 1960, 1962, 1963, 1968, 1971, 1972, 1973, 1975, 1977, 1995 by the Lockman Foundation. Used by permission (www.Lockman.org)

The NASB uses italic to indicate words that have been added for clarification. Citations are shown with large capital letters.

Published by Michael Harvey Koplitz

Acknowledgments

This work could not have been accomplished without Dr. Anne Davis, who taught me Ancient Bible (Hebraic) study methods, and my two study partners, Rev. Dr. Robert Cook and Pastor Sandra Koplitz. We know the journey has just started and will last a lifetime. The discovery of the depths of God's Word is waiting for us to find.

Michael Harvey Koplitz

Table of Contents

Introduction *7*
The main differences between the Greek method and Hebraic method of teaching *9*
Micah Chapter One *17*
Micah Chapter Two *31*
Micah Chapter 3 .... *41*
Micah Chapter Four *49*
Micah Chapter Five *59*
Micah Chapter Six *67*
Micah Chapter Seven *75*
Bibliography *87*

Michael Harvey Koplitz

Introduction

While I was attending Seminary earning my M. Div. degree, I questioned what the instructors and reference books, which were required, were saying about the Scriptures. One idea being offered then was that the Bible was full of errors and not factual. I found that attitude disturbing for Seminary instructors to be teaching. After all, the Seminary experience is to train pastors to go out into God's world and preach the Bible. How can you preach the Bible if you believe what these instructors are teaching? The methods that were being taught to examine the Bible just seemed inaccurate to me.

After graduating from Seminary, I spent a lot of time reading different views about the Bible. I eventually reached the Zohar. This collection of midrashim are considered the secret work of the Torah, according to Kabbalists. In addition, I read quite a bit about Messianic Judaism. Their view of the Bible is quite different from the Seminary view.

I decided that the biblical interpretation that was being taught in Seminary was not the biblical interpretation the people heard when Jesus Christ (whose Hebraic name is Yeshua) preached. I went on a quest to learn what the people of Yeshua's day heard, and what they thought when the Scriptures were read. This quest led me to Dr. Anne Davis and The Bible Learning University. Dr. Davis was in search of the same thing I was searching. She had made many discoveries that helped me in my quest. I earned the Ph.D. degree from The Bible Learning University in Hebraic Studies in Christianity concentrating on ancient Bible Studies methods.

Finally, I found someone who believed that the church has placed almost 1900 years of their theological ideas about the Scriptures and in many places possibly distorting its original meaning. What is also important to hear is that the basic tenants of Yeshua as God's Messiah, my Lord and Savior, are in the Bible. My faith in Yeshua is stronger now that I have learned from Dr. Davis how to study the Scriptures in the same manner that the people did in Yeshua's day.

I have included a couple of articles that describe the differences between Greek learning methods and Hebraic learning methods. Please do not skip by them, unless you are familiar with ancient Bible student method, as irrelevant because if you do then the analysis and commentary that follows may become difficult for you to understand.

Our God is vast and infinite and so is His Word. May God bless you in your discovery of what God's Word is about.

The main differences between the Greek method and Hebraic method of teaching

Once you are aware of the two teaching styles, you will determine if you are in a class or reading a book, whether the analysis and/or teaching method is in a Greek or Hebraic method. In the Greek method, the instructor is right because of advanced knowledge. In the college situation, it is because the professor has his/her Ph.D. in some area of study, so one assumes that he or she knows everything about the topic. For example, Rodney Dangerfield played the role of a middle-aged man going to college. His English midterm was to write about Kurt Vonnegut Jr. Since he did not understand any of Vonnegut's books, he hired Vonnegut himself to the write the midterm. When it was returned to him, the English Professor told Dangerfield that whoever wrote the paper knew nothing about Vonnegut. This is an example of the Greek method of teaching. Did the Ph.D. English professor think she knew more about Vonnegut's writings than Vonnegut did?[1]

In the Greek teaching method, the professor or the instructor claims to be the authority. If you are attending a Bible study class and the class leader says "I will teach you the only way to understand this biblical book," consider the implications. This method is common since most seminaries and Bible colleges teach a Greek method of learning, which is the same method the church has been using for centuries.

Hebraic teaching methods are different. The teacher wants the students to challenge what they hear. It is through questioning that a student can learn. In addition, the teacher wants his/her students to excel to a point where the student becomes the teacher.

---

[1] *Back to School*. Performed by Rodney Dangerfield. Hollywood: CA: Paper Clip Productions, 1986. DVD.

It is said that if two rabbis come together to discuss a passage of Scripture, the result will be at least ten different opinions. All points of view are acceptable as long as the points can be supported by biblical evidence. It is permissible and encouraged for students to have multiple opinions. There is a depth to God's Word, and God wants us to find all of His messages that are placed in the Scriptures.

Seeking the meaning of the Scriptures beyond the literal meaning is essential to fully understanding God's Word.[2] The Greek method of learning the Scriptures has prevailed over the centuries. One problem is that only the literal interpretation of Scripture was often viewed as valid, as prompted by Martin Luther's "sola literalis" meaning that only the literal interpretation of Scripture was valid. The Fundamentalist movements of today are based on the literal interpretation of the Scripture. Therefore, they do not believe that God placed any deeper, hidden, or secret meanings in the Word.

The students of the Scriptures who learn through Hebraic training and understanding have drawn a different conclusion. The Hebrew language itself leads to different possible interpretations because of the construction of the language. The Hebraic method of Bible study opens up avenues of thought about God's revelations in the Scripture that may have never been considered. A question may be raised about the Scripture being studied for which there may not be an immediate answer. If so, it becomes the responsibility of the learners to uncover the meaning. Also, remember that multiple opinions about the meaning of Scripture are also acceptable if they can be supported by Scripture.

---

[2] Davis, Anne Kimball. *The Synoptic Gospels*. MP3. Albuquerque: NM: BibleInteract, 2012.

Methodology

The method employed is to use First Century Scripture study methods integrated with the customs and culture of Yeshua's day to examine the Hebrew and Christian Scriptures, thus gathering a deeper understanding by learning the Scriptures in the way the people of Yeshua's day did.

In typical Rabbinic tradition, I had two study partners. Each one served a different function by looking at the research as I put it together. Rev. Dr. Robert Cook, D. Min., an ordained Elder in the United Methodist Church, has been a study partner in different areas of theology and church leadership. He became interested in Hebraic studies when I started sharing Zohar and Midrash with him. He also completed the entire Disciple program as a student and teacher. My second study partner is my wife, Sandra Koplitz, MS. Sandy and I took the instruction class on teaching the Disciple Bible study program and she takes part in the Zohar study group. Sandy is a licensed local pastor in the United Methodist Church.

The Process of Discovery

I have titled the method of analyzing a passage of Scripture in a Hebraic manner the "Process of Discovery." This method was developed by the author, bringing together the various areas of linguistic and cultural understanding. There are several sections to the process, and not all the sections apply to every passage of Scripture. The overall result of developing this process is to give the reader a framework into the ideas being presented.

The "Process of Discovery" starts with a Scripture passage. If the passage is in a poetic form, it is identified. Possible poetic techniques include parallelism, chiastic structures, and repetition. Formatting the passage in its poetic form allows the reader to visualize what the first century CE listener was hearing. The chiasms are labeled by their corresponding sections, for example: A, B, C, B', A'. Not all passages of the Scriptures have a poetic form.

The next step is to "question the narrative," which is accomplished by assuming the reader knows nothing about the passage. Therefore, the questions go from the simple to the complex. The next task is to identify any linguistic patterns. Linguistic patterns include, but are not limited to: irony, simile, metaphor, symbolism, idioms, hyperbole, figurative language, personification, and allegory.

Any translation inconsistencies discovered between the English NASB version and either the Hebrew or Greek versions are identified. Sometimes a Hebrew or Greek word can be translated in more than one way. Inconsistencies also can be created by the translation committee, which may have used traditional language instead of the actual translation. The decision of the translation committee can be found in the Preface or Introduction to the Bible. Perhaps some inconsistencies were intentionally added to convey some deeper meaning meaning therefore, the inconsistencies need to be examined.

Echoes of the Hebrew Scriptures in the Christian Scripture are identified. This occurs when a passage from the Hebrew Scripture is used in the Christian Scripture or when a Mitzvot is directly discussed in the Christian Scriptures.[3] In addition, echoes can be found when Torah (Genesis through Deuteronomy) passages are used in other Hebrew Bible books. In addition to echoes, cross references are listed. A cross

---

[3] Mitzvot are the 613 commandments found in the Torah that please God. There are positive and negative commandments. The list was first development by Maimonides. The full list can be found at: ttp://www.jewfaq.org/613.htm.

reference is a reference to another verse in the Scripture which can assist the reader to understand the verse that is being read.

The names of persons mentioned in the passage are listed. Many of the Hebrew names have meaning and may be associated with places or actions. Jewish parents used to name their children based on what they felt God had in store for their child. An example of this is Abraham, whose original name was Abram, and was changed to mean eternal father (in this case Abram's name was changed by God to Abraham, showing a function he was to perform). When the Hebrew Bible gives names, many of the occurrences will show something special to the reader/listener. The same importance can hold true for the names of places. The time to travel between places can supply insight to the event.

Keywords are identified in a verse when they are important to an understanding of that passage. There are no rules for selecting the keywords. Searching for other occurrences of the keywords in Scripture in a concordance is necessary to understand how the word was being used; this must be done in either Hebrew or Greek, not in English. A classic Hebraic approach is to find the usage of a word in the Scripture by finding other verses that contain the word. The usage of a word, in its original language, is discovered by searching the Scripture in the Scripture's language. The verses that contain the word being researched are identified and a pattern for the usage of the word is discerned. Each verse is examined to see what the usage of the word is which, may reveal a pattern for the word's usage. For Hebrew words, the first usage of the word in the Scripture, especially if used in the Torah, is important. For the Greek words, the Christian Scriptures are used to determining the word usage in the Scripture. Sometimes finding the equivalent Greek word in the Septuagint and then analyzing its usage in Hebrew can be very helpful.

The Rules of Hillel for Bible understanding can be used when applicable. Hillel was a Torah scholar who lived shortly before Yeshua's day. Hillel developed several rules for Torah students to interpret the Scriptures which are referred to as halachic midrash. In several cases, these rules are helpful in the analysis of the Scripture.

After the linguistic analysis is complete, an examination of the cultural implications will be examined. The culture is important because it is not specifically referenced in the biblical narratives as showed earlier.

From linguistic analysis and the cultural understanding, it is possible to get a deeper meaning of the Scripture beyond the literal meaning of the plaintext. That is what the listeners of Yeshua's time were doing. They put the linguistics and the culture together without even having to contemplate it. They did it.

This will lead to a conclusion or a set of conclusions about what the passage is discussing. Most of the time the Hebraic analysis leads to the desire for a deeper analysis in order to fully understand what Yeshua was discussing or what was happening to Him. Whatever the result, a new deeper understanding of the Scripture will be obtained.

The components of the Process of Discovery are:
- Linguistics Section
  - Linguistic Structure of the Scripture
  - Discussion
  - Questioning the Passage
  - Verse Comparison on citations or proof text

- Translation inconsistencies
- People's names
- Name of places
- Word Study
- Scripture cross references
- Echoes
- Rules of Hillel
- Main/Center Point

Culture Section
- Discussion
- Questioning the passage culturally

Culture and Linguistics Section
- Discussion

Only the sections that are applicable to each chapter are presented.

Micah Chapter One

Language

New American Standard 1995	Hebrew	Septuagint (Greek Version translated)
¹ The word of the LORD which came to Micah of Moresheth in the days of Jotham, Ahaz and Hezekiah, kings of Judah, which he saw concerning Samaria and Jerusalem. ² Hear, O peoples, all of you; Listen, O earth and all it contains, And let the Lord GOD be a witness against you, The Lord from His holy temple. ³ For behold, the LORD is coming forth from His place. He will come down and tread on the high places of the earth. ⁴ The mountains will melt under Him And the valleys will be split, Like wax before the fire, Like water poured down a steep place. ⁵ All this is for the rebellion of Jacob And for the sins of the house of Israel. What is the rebellion of Jacob? Is it not Samaria? What is the high place of Judah? Is it not Jerusalem? ⁶ For I will make Samaria a heap of ruins in the open	₁ דְּבַר־יְהוָה׀ אֲשֶׁר הָיָה אֶל־מִיכָה הַמֹּרַשְׁתִּי בִּימֵי יוֹתָם אָחָז יְחִזְקִיָּה מַלְכֵי יְהוּדָה אֲשֶׁר־חָזָה עַל־שֹׁמְרוֹן וִירוּשָׁלָםִ׃ ² שִׁמְעוּ עַמִּים כֻּלָּם הַקְשִׁיבִי אֶרֶץ וּמְלֹאָהּ וִיהִי אֲדֹנָי יְהוִה בָּכֶם לְעֵד אֲדֹנָי מֵהֵיכַל קָדְשׁוֹ׃ ³ כִּי־הִנֵּה יְהוָה יֹצֵא מִמְּקוֹמוֹ וְיָרַד וְדָרַךְ עַל־(בָּמוֹתֵי) [בָּמֳתֵי] אָרֶץ׃ ⁴ וְנָמַסּוּ הֶהָרִים תַּחְתָּיו וְהָעֲמָקִים יִתְבַּקָּעוּ כַּדּוֹנַג מִפְּנֵי הָאֵשׁ כְּמַיִם מֻגָּרִים בְּמוֹרָד׃ ⁵ בְּפֶשַׁע יַעֲקֹב כָּל־זֹאת וּבְחַטֹּאות בֵּית יִשְׂרָאֵל מִי־פֶשַׁע יַעֲקֹב הֲלוֹא שֹׁמְרוֹן וּמִי בָּמוֹת יְהוּדָה הֲלוֹא יְרוּשָׁלָםִ׃ ⁶ וְשַׂמְתִּי שֹׁמְרוֹן לְעִי הַשָּׂדֶה לְמַטָּעֵי כָרֶם וְהִגַּרְתִּי לַגַּי אֲבָנֶיהָ וִיסֹדֶיהָ אֲגַלֶּה׃ ⁷ וְכָל־פְּסִילֶיהָ יֻכַּתּוּ וְכָל־אֶתְנַנֶּיהָ יִשָּׂרְפוּ בָאֵשׁ וְכָל־עֲצַבֶּיהָ אָשִׂים שְׁמָמָה כִּי מֵאֶתְנַן זוֹנָה קִבָּצָה וְעַד־אֶתְנַן זוֹנָה יָשׁוּבוּ׃ ⁸ עַל־זֹאת אֶסְפְּדָה וְאֵילִילָה אֵילְכָה (שֵׁילָל) [שׁוֹלָל] וְעָרוֹם אֶעֱשֶׂה מִסְפֵּד כַּתַּנִּים וְאֵבֶל כִּבְנוֹת יַעֲנָה׃ ⁹ כִּי אֲנוּשָׁה מַכּוֹתֶיהָ כִּי־בָאָה עַד־יְהוּדָה נָגַע עַד־שַׁעַר עַמִּי עַד־יְרוּשָׁלָםִ׃ ¹⁰ בְּגַת אַל־תַּגִּידוּ בָּכוֹ אַל־תִּבְכּוּ בְּבֵית לְעַפְרָה עָפָר (הִתְפַּלָּשְׁתִּי) [הִתְפַּלָּשִׁי]׃	And the word of the Lord came to Michaeas the son of Morasthi, in the days of Joatham, and Achaz, and Ezekias, kings of Juda, concerning what he saw regarding Samaria and Jerusalem. ² Hear *these* words, ye people; and let the earth give heed, and all that are in it: and the Lord God shall be among you for a testimony, the Lord out of his holy habitation. ³ For, behold, the Lord comes forth out of his place, and will come down, and will go upon the high places of the earth. ⁴ And the mountains shall be shaken under him, and the valleys shall melt like wax before the fire, and as water rushing down a declivity. ⁵ All these *calamities are* for the transgression of Jacob, and for the sin of the house of Israel. What is the transgression of Jacob? *is it* not Samaria? and what is the sin of the house of Juda? *is it* not Jerusalem?

country, Planting places for a vineyard. I will pour her stones down into the valley And will lay bare her foundations. ⁷ All of her idols will be smashed, All of her earnings will be burned with fire And all of her images I will make desolate, For she collected *them* from a harlot's earnings, And to the earnings of a harlot they will return. ⁸ Because of this I must lament and wail, I must go barefoot and naked; I must make a lament like the jackals And a mourning like the ostriches. ⁹ For her wound is incurable, For it has come to Judah; It has reached the gate of my people, *Even* to Jerusalem. ¹⁰ Tell it not in Gath, Weep not at all. At Beth-le-aphrah roll yourself in the dust. ¹¹ Go on your way, inhabitant of Shaphir, in shameful nakedness. The inhabitant of Zaanan does not escape. The lamentation of Beth-ezel: "He will take from you its support." ¹² For the inhabitant of Maroth Becomes weak waiting for good, Because a calamity has come down	¹¹ עִבְרִ֨י לָכֶ֜ם יוֹשֶׁ֤בֶת שָׁפִיר֙ עֶרְיָה־בֹ֔שֶׁת לֹ֤א יָֽצְאָה֙ יוֹשֶׁ֣בֶת צַֽאֲנָ֔ן מִסְפַּד֙ בֵּ֣ית הָאֵ֔צֶל יִקַּ֥ח מִכֶּ֖ם עֶמְדָּתֽוֹ׃ ¹² כִּי־חָ֥לָֽה לְט֖וֹב יוֹשֶׁ֣בֶת מָר֑וֹת כִּי־יָ֤רַד רָע֙ מֵאֵ֣ת יְהוָ֔ה לְשַׁ֖עַר יְרוּשָׁלִָֽם׃ ¹³ רְתֹ֧ם הַמֶּרְכָּבָ֛ה לָרֶ֖כֶשׁ יוֹשֶׁ֣בֶת לָכִ֑ישׁ רֵאשִׁ֨ית חַטָּ֥את הִיא֙ לְבַת־צִיּ֔וֹן כִּי־בָ֥ךְ נִמְצְא֖וּ פִּשְׁעֵ֥י יִשְׂרָאֵֽל׃ ¹⁴ לָכֵן֙ תִּתְּנִ֣י שִׁלּוּחִ֔ים עַ֖ל מוֹרֶ֣שֶׁת גַּ֑ת בָּתֵּ֤י אַכְזִיב֙ לְאַכְזָ֔ב לְמַלְכֵ֖י יִשְׂרָאֵֽל׃ ¹⁵ עֹ֗ד הַיֹּרֵשׁ֙ אָ֣בִי לָ֔ךְ יוֹשֶׁ֖בֶת מָֽרֵשָׁ֑ה עַד־עֲדֻלָּ֥ם יָב֖וֹא כְּב֥וֹד יִשְׂרָאֵֽל׃ ¹⁶ קָרְחִ֣י וָגֹ֔זִּי עַל־בְּנֵ֖י תַּעֲנוּגָ֑יִךְ הַרְחִ֤בִי קָרְחָתֵךְ֙ כַּנֶּ֔שֶׁר כִּ֥י גָל֖וּ מִמֵּֽךְ׃ ס	⁶ Therefore I will make Samaria *as* a store-house of the fruits of the field, and *as* a planting of a vineyard: and I will utterly demolish her stones, and I will expose her foundations. ⁷ And they shall cut in pieces all the graven images, and all that she has hired they shall burn with fire, and I will utterly destroy all her idols: because she has gathered of the hires of fornication, and of the hires of fornication has she amassed *wealth*. ⁸ Therefore shall she lament and wail, she shall go barefooted, and *being* naked she shall make lamentation as *that* of serpents, and mourning as of the daughters of sirens. ⁹ For her plague has become grievous; for it has come even to Juda; and has reached to the gate of my people, even to Jerusalem. ¹⁰ Ye that are in Geth, exalt not yourselves, and ye Enakim, do not rebuild from *the ruins of* the house in derision: sprinkle dust *in the place of* your laughter. ¹¹ The inhabitant of Sennaar, fairly inhabiting her cities, came not forth to mourn for the house next to her: she shall receive of you the stroke of grief.

from the LORD To the gate of Jerusalem. ¹³ Harness the chariot to the team of horses, O inhabitant of Lachish-- She was the beginning of sin To the daughter of Zion-- Because in you were found The rebellious acts of Israel. ¹⁴ Therefore you will give parting gifts On behalf of Moresheth-gath; The houses of Achzib *will* become a deception To the kings of Israel. ¹⁵ Moreover, I will bring on you The one who takes possession, O inhabitant of Mareshah. The glory of Israel will enter Adullam. ¹⁶ Make yourself bald and cut off your hair, Because of the children of your delight; Extend your baldness like the eagle, For they will go from you into exile.		¹² Who has begun *to act* for good to her that dwells in sorrow? for calamities have come down from the Lord upon the gates of Jerusalem, ¹³ *even* a sound of chariots and horsemen: the inhabitants of Lachis, she is the leader of sin to the daughter of Sion: for in thee were found the transgressions of Israel. ¹⁴ Therefore shall he cause men to be sent forth as far as the inheritance of Geth, *even* vain houses; they are become vanity to the kings of Israel; ¹⁵ until they bring the heirs, O inhabitant of Lachis: the inheritance shall reach to Odollam, *even* the glory of the daughter of Israel. ¹⁶ Shave thine hair, and make thyself bald for thy delicate children; increase thy widowhood as an eagle; for *thy people* are gone into captivity from thee.

Process of Discovery

Linguistics Section

Linguistic Structure

A ¹ The word of the LORD which came *to* Micah of Moresheth in the days of Jotham, Ahaz *and* Hezekiah, kings of Judah, which he saw **concerning Samaria and Jerusalem**.

² Hear, O peoples, all of you; Listen, O earth and all it contains, And let the Lord GOD be a witness against you, The Lord from His holy temple. ³ For behold, the LORD is coming forth from His place. He will come down and tread on the high places of the earth. ⁴ The **mountains will melt** under Him And the valleys will be split, Like wax before the fire, Like water poured down a steep place.

A' ⁵ All this is for the rebellion of Jacob And for the sins of the house of Israel. What is the rebellion of Jacob? Is it not **Samaria**? What is the high place of Judah? Is it not **Jerusalem**?

⁶ For I will make **Samaria a heap of ruins** in the open country, Planting places for a vineyard. I will pour her stones down into the valley And will lay bare her foundations. ⁷ All of her idols will be smashed, All of her earnings will be burned with fire And all of her images I will make desolate, For she collected *them* from a harlot's earnings, And to the earnings of a harlot they will return.

[Declaration] ⁸ Because of this I must lament and wail, I must go barefoot and naked; I must make a lament like the jackals And a mourning like the ostriches. ⁹ For her wound is incurable, For it has come to Judah; It has reached the gate of my people, *Even* to Jerusalem.

[Gath] ¹⁰ Tell it not in Gath, Weep not at all. At Beth-le-aphrah roll yourself in the dust.[1]

[Shaphir] ¹¹ Go on your way, inhabitant of Shaphir, in shameful nakedness. The inhabitant of Zaanan does not escape. The lamentation of Beth-ezel: "He will take from you its support." ¹² For the inhabitant of Maroth Becomes weak waiting for good, Because a calamity has come down from the LORD To the gate of Jerusalem. ¹

[Lachish] ³ Harness the chariot to the team of horses, O inhabitant of Lachish-- She was the beginning of sin To the daughter of Zion-- Because in you were found The rebellious acts of Israel. ¹⁴ Therefore you will give parting gifts On behalf of Moresheth-gath; The houses of Achzib *will* become a deception To the kings of Israel.

[Mareshah] ¹⁵ Moreover, I will bring on you The one who takes possession, O inhabitant of Mareshah. The glory of Israel will enter Adullam. ¹⁶ Make yourself bald and cut off your hair, Because of the children of your delight; Extend your baldness like the eagle, For they will go from you into exile. (Mic. 1:1-16 NAU)

Discussion

The chapter begins with a short chiasm in which the LORD told Micah that the major portion of his prophecy was to be that the LORD would destroy the land of Samaria and Jerusalem. This is followed by specific prophecies directed toward four cities.

Questioning the Passage

1. What does it mean to have the LORD being a witness against you? (v. 2)

    Micah tells the people that he is prophesying in the LORD's name against the evil ways of the people.

2. Where is the LORD's place? (v. 3)

    The Targum[4] of Micah tells us that the LORD will appear from the place of the Shekinah, which is the Temple at Jerusalem.[5]

3. What does it mean for the LORD to tread on the high places? (v. 3)

    When examining this verse, with verse four, the LORD will come out of His house in Jerusalem and will cause destruction of the land as a part of the execution of judgment.

---

[4] The Targum is an Aramaic translation which was created by rabbis starting after the Babylonian Exile. The translation also includes commentary which was inserted to help the readers to understand God's Word.
[5] Cathcart, Kevin J., and R. P. Gordon. The Targum of the Minor Prophets. Wilmington, DE: M. Glazier, 1989. 113.

4. How will the valleys be split? (v. 4)

    The LORD will be "walking" on the mountains and in valleys. The mountains will be destroyed and the valleys will be split by the LORD walking on them. Since the mountains are symbolic of the leaders, the valleys could be symbolic of the people of the land.

5. How is Samaria the rebellion of Jacob? (v. 5)

    The Sage Radak[6] said that the house of Jacob is the same as Samaria. In contrast Malbim[7] said that Jacob refers to the Northern Kingdom while Judah refers to the Southern Kingdom. The rebellion is the idolatry of the Northern Kingdom when they established golden calves in the Kingdom and told the people to pray to these idols. Samaria is another name for the Northern Kingdom. Therefore, Malbim's explanation is possibly more accurate.

6. Why is Jerusalem called a high place of Judah? (v. 5)

    Altars were constructed on high places because ancient people believed that the closer one was to the firmament (the sky), the closer one was to God. Therefore, the high places were mountain tops. The city of Jerusalem was built on a mountaintop.

---

[6] The great grammarian and scholar Rabbi David Kimchi, was a member of a famous family which greatly enriched our Talmudic and Hebrew literature. It was said of this family, (Where there is no *Kemach* - flour [bread] there can be no learning [Torah]), "were it not for the Kimchis, there would be no Torah," a saying based on the similarity of the name Kimchi with the Hebrew word *Kemach*. Source: "Rabbi David Kimchi - RaDaK - (4920-4995; 1160-1235)." - Jewish History. Source: Mindel, Nissan. Rabbi David Kimchi - RaDaK. Brooklyn, N.Y.: Kehot Publication Society.

[7] Russian rabbi, preacher, and Hebraist; born at Volochisk, Volhynia, in 1809; died at Kiev Sept. 18, 1879. The name "Malbim" is derived from the initials of his name (מלבים), and became his family name by frequent usage. Malbim was educated in Hebrew and Talmud by his father and by his stepfather (R. Löb of Volochisk). He showed unusual talent from his early childhood, and his works indicate that he had a considerable knowledge of secular sciences. Source: Cohen, Simon. "Malbim." In The Universal Jewish Encyclopedia: An Authoritative and Popular Presentation of Jews and Judaism since the Earliest times. New York: Universal Jewish Encyclopedia, 1948.

7. What were the earnings of Samaria (v. 7)

    When the Scripture refers to a harlot's earning, it means that the nation used idolatry to support itself financially (for example, creating and selling idols of wood, stone or metal). The idolatry of the nation made everything Samaria did sinful.

8. What were the parting gifts? (v. 14)

    Gifts to Achzib[8] should get the people to assist Judah in any upcoming attacks. Micah was trying to motivate the people to destroy Achzib because this city was going to be a continual problem.

9. What was the glory of Israel? (v. 15)

    The glory of Israel is its protection from the LORD through the Shekinah.

Metaphors

1. How will the mountains melt under the LORD? (v. 4)

    This a metaphor reminds us of fire melting wax (Abarbanel[9]). The mountains are the leaders of the nations, Northern and Southern Kingdom. Fire describes the wrath of God.[10] The LORD will destroy the Kings and leaders of the Northern and Southern Kingdom.

---

[8] Achzib was a city in the Judean plain and was also the name of a Philistine city. Most likely Micah is referring to the Philistine city. The Israelites never captured the costal plain where the Philistine's lived. The Philistines were a continuous problem for Israel.

[9] **Abrabanel (Abravanel). Isaac ben Judah** (1437–1508), Jewish statesman, commentator, and philosopher. He succeeded his father as treasurer to the Portuguese king Alfonso V, but was compelled to flee to Spain when he was suspected of participating in rebellion against his successor. Source: Bowker, John. "Isaac Abravanel." In *The Concise Oxford Dictionary of World Religions*. Oxford: Oxford University Press, 2005.

[10] Scherman, Nosson, Meir Zlotowitz, Sheah Brander, and Menachem Davis. "Micah." In The Prophets: The Later Prophets with a Commentary Anthologized from the Rabbinic Writings. Brooklyn, NY: Mesorah Publications, 2013. p. 242.

Symbols

1. What is the symbolism of going barefoot and naked? (v. 8)

    "To go barefoot was a sign of great distress (Isaiah 20:2 Isaiah 20:3 Isaiah 20:4), or of some great calamity having fallen on a person (2 Samuel 15:30)."[11] However, in the Targum of Micah, the verse says "naked and in chains." It is referring to what was going to happen to the people of the Northern Kingdom when the Assyrians invaded.[12]

2. What is the symbolism of lamenting like a jackal and mourning like an ostrich? (v. 8)

    Jackals and ostrich make sounds like the wailing of mourners. The people would wail over the judgment that the LORD was going to instill because the people had not changed from their evil ways.

3. What does it mean to roll oneself in dust? (v. 10)

    People in mourning placed ashes on their heads. Rolling in the dust is the same thing. The people would be in mourning because of the amount of death that was to occur when the Assyrians invaded.

4. What does it symbolize to make oneself bald? (v. 16)

    Tearing out a part of one's hair or using a scissor to create the bald patch is a sign of mourning.

5. What is the symbolism of the eagle? (v. 16)

    Eagles shed most of their feathers from time to time. The symbolism of the eagle is symbolic of men tearing their hair out because of their mourning.

---

[11] "Barefoot Definition and Meaning - Bible Dictionary." Bible Study Tools. Accessed February 01, 2017. http://www.biblestudytools.com/dictionary/barefoot/.
[12] Cathcart, Kevin J., and R. P. Gordon. The Targum of the Minor Prophets. Wilmington, DE: M. Glazier, 1989. 114.

People's names

1. מִיכָה *Mikah* **Meaning:** the name of several Israelites

    "Prophet; author of the sixth book in the collection known as "The Twelve Minor Prophets" (Mic. i. 1). The name of the prophet appears to be a shortened form of מיכיה , "Micaiah" (= "Who is like Yhwh?"), and is so written in Jer. xxvi. 18 (comp. also Micah No. 2). The only data concerning Micah are those given in the superscription of the book bearing his name. He was a Morasthite[13]; , a native of Moreshethgath (Mic. i. 14); and he prophesied in the days of Jotham, Ahaz, and Hezekiah, kings of Judah—a period covering at the most fifty-nine years (756-697 B.C.)."[14]

2. יוֹתָם *Yotham* **Meaning:** 'the LORD is perfect,' the name of several Israelites

    "Son of Uzziah or Azariah; tenth king of Judah (751 to 735 B.C.). His father sacrilegiously offered incense in the Temple (II Chron. xxvi. 16-21) and was smitten with leprosy. He was thus compelled to dwell apart from the people, and for nearly fourteen years Jotham was regent, or, in reality, king over Judah. He inherited a strong government, well officered and administered. He himself is said to have built the upper gate of the house of Yhwh and to have avoided the rashness which allowed his father to enter the Temple (II Chron. xxvii. 2)."[15]

3. אָחָז *Achaz* **Meaning:** 'he has grasped,' name of a King

    "Son of King Jotham. His reign is memorable as that in which Judah first became vassal to Assyria, and Assyrian (Babylonian) modes of worship were first introduced into the official worship at Jerusalem."[16]

4. חִזְקִיָּה *Chizqiyyah* or חִזְקִיָּהוּ *Chizqiyyahu* or יְחִזְקִיָּה *Yechizqiyyah* or יְחִזְקִיָּהוּ *Yechizqiyyahu*

    Meaning: 'Yah has strengthened,' a king of Judah, also several other Israelites, in English is Hezekiah.

    "Son of Ahaz and Abi or Abijah; ascended the throne at the age of twenty-five and reigned twenty-nine years (II Kings xviii. 1-2; II Chron. xxix. 1). Hezekiah was the opposite of his father, Ahaz; and no king of Judah, among either his predecessors or his successors, could, it is said, be compared to him (II Kings xviii. 5). His first act

---

[13] Micah was born in the city of Moresheth.
[14] "JewishEncyclopedia.com." *MICAH - JewishEncyclopedia.com*. N.p., n.d. Web. 14 Feb. 2017."
[15] IBID.
[16] IBID.

was to repair the Temple, which had been closed during the reign of Ahaz. To this end he reorganized the services of the priests and Levites, purged the Temple and its vessels, and opened it with imposing sacrifices (II Chron. xxix. 3-36)."[17]

5. יַעֲקֹב *Yaaqob* **Meaning:** a son of Isaac, also his descendants. Patriarch of Israel. He was the second son of Isaac.

Name of places

1. מוֹרַשְׁתִּי *Morashti* **Meaning:** inhabitants of Moresheth-gath

2. יְרוּשָׁלַם *Yerushalaim* or יְרוּשָׁלַיִם *Yerushalayim,* capital of the Southern Kingdom

3. יְהוּדָה *Yehudah* **Meaning:** 'praised,' a son of Jacob, also his descendants, a name for the Southern Kingdom

4. גַּת *Gath* **Meaning:** 'wine press,' a Philistine city

5. בֵּית לְעַפְרָה *Beth Leaphrah* **Meaning:** 'house to dust,' a place in Israel

6. שָׁפִיר *Shaphir* **Meaning:** 'beauty,' a place perhaps in Philistia (exact location is not known)

7. צַאֲנָן *Tsaanan* **Meaning:** a place perhaps in the Shephelah of Judah (exact location is not known)

---

[17] IBID.

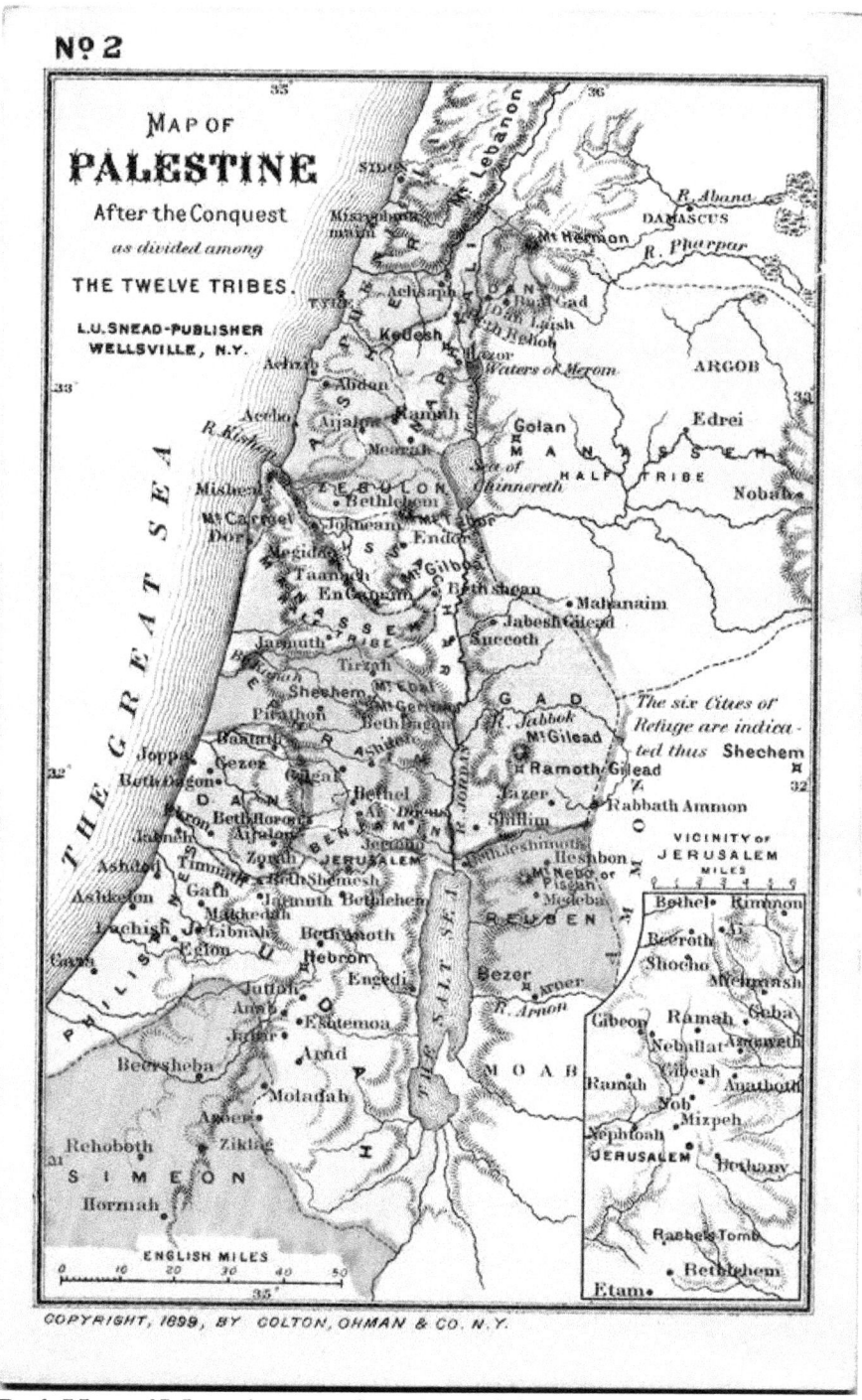

8. בֵּית הָאֵצֶל *Beth Haetsel* **Meaning:** a place in Judah

9. מָרוֹת *Maroth* **Meaning:** a place in Judah

10. לָכִישׁ *Lachish* **Meaning:** a Canaanite city south west of Jerusalem

11. צִיּוֹן *Tsiyyon* **Meaning:** the mountain which Jerusalem is located, also a name for Jerusalem.

12. מוֹרֶשֶׁת גַּת *Moresheth Gath* **Meaning:** 'possession,' a place near Gath

13. מַרֵאשָׁה *Mareshah* or מָרֵשָׁה *Mareshah* **Meaning:** a place in Judah, also two Isr.

14. עֲדֻלָּם *Adullam* **Meaning:** a Canaanite city

Word Study
   N/A

Scripture cross references

Verse 3	Isa 26:21, Amo 4:13
Verse 5	Jer 2:19, Isa 7:9, Amo 8:14, 2Ch 34:3, 2Ch 34:4
Verse 7	Jer 2:19, Isa 7:9, Amo 8:14, 2Ch 34:3, 2Ch 34:4
Verse 8	Isa 32:11, Isa 13:21, Isa 13:22
Verse 12	Isa 59:9-11, Jer 14:19

Main/Center Point

Judgment was coming to the land because of the iniquities of the people.

Culture Section

Discussion

Micah was from the city Mareshah which was located in the kingdom of Judah. His teacher was Isaiah the prophet and he received the Oral Tradition from Isaiah. Micah prophesied during the days of Ahab, the king of the Northern kingdom and during the days of Jotham, Ahaz, and Hezekiah, Kings of the Southern Kingdom.

Micah's name has been abbreviated from Micaiah, which means "who is like unto God." He lived in the eighth century BCE and was the younger contemporary of Hosea and Isaiah. The three have very similar teachings. Micah's book was probably written prior to the fall of Samaria in 721 BCE since there are references to the destruction of Samaria. Micah was a simple peasant who had seen too many evils, oppressions and injustices. He denounced sacrifices because it led to self-righteousness. He admonished his people to implement justice, mercy, and kindness.

Micah warned Judah that it would suffer the same fate as Israel did. As with all the books of the prophets, there is a sign of hope at the end of the book. Micah believed that God's truth and justice would abolish all war and sanctify the people.[18]

Thoughts

Micah lived in the time prior to the Assyrian invasion of the Northern Kingdom of Israel, which wiped out the ten northern tribes. The LORD is clear that had Samaria (the Northern Kingdom) heeded the word of the LORD, the calamity that came upon them would have been prevented. The leadership of the Southern Kingdom was just as corrupt as the North. History tells us that the Assyrians were appeased by King Hezekiah, who also did a massive reform movement to restore worship to the LORD. As per other prophets, Micah pronounced doom for all who did not bow down to God and live their lives by His Word.

---

[18] Errico, Rocco A., and George M. Lamsa. "Micah Chapter One." In Aramaic Light on Ezekiel, Daniel, and the Minor Prophets: A Commentary Based on the Aramaic Language and Ancient Near Eastern Customs. Smyma, GA: Noohra Foundation, 2012.

Micah Chapter Two

Language

New American Standard 1995	Hebrew	Septuagint
1 Woe to those who scheme iniquity, Who work out evil on their beds! When morning comes, they do it, For it is in the power of their hands. ² They covet fields and then seize *them*, And houses, and take *them* away. They rob a man and his house, A man and his inheritance. ³ Therefore thus says the LORD, "Behold, I am planning against this family a calamity From which you cannot remove your necks; And you will not walk haughtily, For it will be an evil time. ⁴ "On that day they will take up against you a taunt And utter a bitter lamentation *and* say, 'We are completely destroyed! He exchanges the portion of my people; How He removes it from me! To the apostate He apportions our fields.' ⁵ "Therefore you will have no one stretching a measuring line For you by	הוֹי חֹשְׁבֵי־אָוֶן וּפֹעֲלֵי רָע עַל־מִשְׁכְּבוֹתָם בְּאוֹר הַבֹּקֶר יַעֲשׂוּהָ כִּי יֶשׁ־לְאֵל יָדָם: ² וְחָמְדוּ שָׂדוֹת וְגָזָלוּ וּבָתִּים וְנָשָׂאוּ וְעָשְׁקוּ גֶּבֶר וּבֵיתוֹ וְאִישׁ וְנַחֲלָתוֹ: פ ³ לָכֵן כֹּה אָמַר יְהוָה הִנְנִי חֹשֵׁב עַל־הַמִּשְׁפָּחָה הַזֹּאת רָעָה אֲשֶׁר לֹא־תָמִישׁוּ מִשָּׁם צַוְּארֹתֵיכֶם וְלֹא תֵלְכוּ רוֹמָה כִּי עֵת רָעָה הִיא: ⁴ בַּיּוֹם הַהוּא יִשָּׂא עֲלֵיכֶם מָשָׁל וְנָהָה נְהִי נִהְיָה אָמַר שָׁדוֹד נְשַׁדֻּנוּ חֵלֶק עַמִּי יָמִיר אֵיךְ יָמִישׁ לִי לְשׁוֹבֵב שָׂדֵינוּ יְחַלֵּק: ⁵ לָכֵן לֹא־יִהְיֶה לְךָ מַשְׁלִיךְ חֶבֶל בְּגוֹרָל בִּקְהַל יְהוָה: ⁶ אַל־תַּטִּפוּ יַטִּיפוּן לֹא־יַטִּפוּ לָאֵלֶּה לֹא יִסַּג כְּלִמּוֹת: ⁷ הֶאָמוּר בֵּית־יַעֲקֹב הֲקָצַר רוּחַ יְהוָה אִם־אֵלֶּה מַעֲלָלָיו הֲלוֹא דְבָרַי יֵיטִיבוּ עִם הַיָּשָׁר הוֹלֵךְ: ⁸ וְאֶתְמוּל עַמִּי לְאוֹיֵב יְקוֹמֵם מִמּוּל שַׂלְמָה אֶדֶר תַּפְשִׁטוּן מֵעֹבְרִים בֶּטַח שׁוּבֵי מִלְחָמָה: ⁹ נְשֵׁי עַמִּי תְּגָרְשׁוּן מִבֵּית תַּעֲנֻגֶיהָ מֵעַל עֹלָלֶיהָ תִּקְחוּ הֲדָרִי לְעוֹלָם: ¹⁰ קוּמוּ וּלְכוּ כִּי לֹא־זֹאת הַמְּנוּחָה בַּעֲבוּר טָמְאָה תְּחַבֵּל וְחֶבֶל נִמְרָץ: ¹¹ לוּ־אִישׁ הֹלֵךְ רוּחַ וָשֶׁקֶר כִּזֵּב אַטִּף לְךָ לַיַּיִן וְלַשֵּׁכָר וְהָיָה מַטִּיף הָעָם הַזֶּה:	¹ They meditated troubles, and wrought wickedness on their beds, and they put it in execution with the daylight; for they have not lifted up their hands to God. ² And they desired fields, and plundered orphans, and oppressed families, and spoiled a man and his house, even a man and his inheritance. ³ Therefore thus saith the Lord; Behold, I devise evils against this family, out of which ye shall not lift up your necks, neither shall ye walk upright speedily: for the time is evil. ⁴ In that day shall a parable be taken up against you, and a plaintive lamentation shall be uttered, saying, We are thoroughly miserable: the portion of my people has been measured out with a line, and there was none to hinder him so as to turn him back; your fields have been divided. ⁵ Therefore thou shalt have no one to cast a line for the lot.

lot in the assembly of the LORD. ⁶ 'Do not speak out,' *so* they speak out. *But if* they do not speak out concerning these things, Reproaches will not be turned back. ⁷ "Is it being said, O house of Jacob: 'Is the Spirit of the LORD impatient? Are these His doings?' Do not My words do good To the one walking uprightly? ⁸ "Recently My people have arisen as an enemy-- You strip the robe off the garment From unsuspecting passers-by, *From* those returned from war. ⁹ "The women of My people you evict, Each *one* from her pleasant house. From her children you take My splendor forever. ¹⁰ "Arise and go, For this is no place of rest Because of the uncleanness that brings on destruction, A painful destruction. ¹¹ "If a man walking after wind and falsehood Had told lies *and said*, 'I will speak out to you concerning wine and liquor,' He would be spokesman to this people. ¹² "I will surely assemble all of you, Jacob, I will surely gather the remnant of Israel. I will put them together like sheep in the	¹² אָסֹף אֶאֱסֹף יַעֲקֹב כֻּלָּךְ קַבֵּץ אֲקַבֵּץ שְׁאֵרִית יִשְׂרָאֵל יָחַד אֲשִׂימֶנּוּ כְּצֹאן בָּצְרָה כְּעֵדֶר בְּתוֹךְ הַדָּבְרוֹ תְּהִימֶנָה מֵאָדָם׃ ¹³ עָלָה הַפֹּרֵץ לִפְנֵיהֶם פָּרְצוּ וַיַּעֲבֹרוּ שַׁעַר וַיֵּצְאוּ בוֹ וַיַּעֲבֹר מַלְכָּם לִפְנֵיהֶם וַיהוָה בְּרֹאשָׁם׃ פ	⁶ Weep not with tears in the assembly of the Lord, neither let *any* weep for these things; for he shall not remove the reproaches, ⁷ who says, The house of Jacob has provoked the Spirit of the Lord; are not these his practices? Are not the Lord's words right with him? and have they not proceeded correctly? ⁸ Even beforetime my people withstood *him* as an enemy against his peace; they have stripped off his skin to remove hope *in* the conflict of war. ⁹ The leaders of my people shall be cast forth from their luxurious houses; they are rejected because of their evil practices; draw ye near to the everlasting mountains. ¹⁰ Arise thou, and depart; for this is not thy rest because of uncleanness: ye have been utterly destroyed; ¹¹ ye have fled, no one pursuing *you*: *thy* spirit has framed falsehood, it has dropped on thee for wine and strong drink. But it shall come to pass, *that* out of the dropping of this people, ¹² Jacob shall be completely gathered with all *his people*: I will surely receive the remnant of

fold; Like a flock in the midst of its pasture They will be noisy with men. ¹³ "The breaker goes up before them; They break out, pass through the gate and go out by it. So their king goes on before them, And the LORD at their head." (Mic. 2:1-13 NAU)		Israel; I will cause them to return together, as sheep in trouble, as a flock in the midst of their fold: they shall rush forth from among men through the breach made before them: ¹³ they have broken through, and passed the gate, and gone out by it: and their king has gone out before them, and the Lord shall lead them.

Process of Discovery
Linguistics Section

Linguistic Structure

A [robbery] [1] Woe to those who scheme iniquity, Who work out evil on their beds! When morning comes, they do it, For it is in the power of their hands. [2] They covet fields and then seize *them*, And houses, and take *them* away. They rob a man and his house, A man and his inheritance.

> **B [judgment executed]** [3] Therefore thus says the LORD, "Behold, I am planning against this family a calamity From which you cannot remove your necks; And you will not walk haughtily, For it will be an evil time. [4] "On that day they will take up against you a taunt And utter a bitter lamentation *and* say, 'We are completely destroyed! He exchanges the portion of my people; How He removes it from me! To the apostate He apportions our fields.' [5] "Therefore you will have no one stretching a measuring line For you by lot in the assembly of the LORD. [6] 'Do not speak out,' *so* they speak out. *But if* they do not speak out concerning these things, Reproaches will not be turned back.

A' [robbery] [7] "Is it being said, O house of Jacob: 'Is the Spirit of the LORD impatient? Are these His doings?' Do not My words do good To the one walking uprightly? [8] "Recently My people have arisen as an enemy-- You strip the robe off the garment From unsuspecting passers-by, *From* those returned from war. [9] "The women of My people you evict, Each *one* from her pleasant house. From her children you take My splendor forever.

> **B' [judgment executed]** [10] "Arise and go, For this is no place of rest Because of the uncleanness that brings on destruction, A painful destruction. [11] "If a man walking after wind and falsehood Had told lies *and said*, 'I will speak out to you concerning wine and liquor,' He would be spokesman to this people. [12] "I will surely assemble all of you, Jacob, I will surely gather the remnant of Israel. I will put them together like sheep in the fold; Like a flock in the midst of its pasture They will be noisy with men. [13] "The breaker goes up before them; They break out, pass through the gate and go out by it. So their king goes on before them, And the LORD at their head."

Discussion

This chapter is a simple A-B-A'-B' chiasm. The chapter discusses a crime and the execution of judgment.

Questioning the Passage

1. What does it mean to work out evil on your bed?

    The prophet Micah describes the evil that was happening in the land. The Targum tells us that those who plan on their beds are those who are planning to do evil and that which is wicked. Another way to look at evil on your bed is that those who wish to be wicked not only plan but also execute their plans during the day. When lying in bed, one would usually contemplate and reflect upon the Scriptures as seen in Psalm 4:5. Instead, they are scheming because they are evil (from the Sage Radak). God does not punish for thinking about evil but with the people in Micah's time, their evil thinking was executed the very next morning.[19]

2. What does it mean to remove your necks? (v. 3)

    The reference to the necks of the people is because evil is like a heavy yoke that is placed upon the neck and the people cannot remove it. It also tells us that the punishment God will place upon the people can only be removed by God.

3. What does it mean to "exchange a portion of my people" in verse four?

    The portion that is being referred to is the land that the people received as part of an inheritance, which Moses promised to the people of God.

4. What is a measuring line? (v. 5)

    A measuring line was used when one wanted to sell a portion of his property or his land. Micah is telling us that when the people are punished, they cannot decide what part of their property they will lose, but they will lose everything, including their land.

---

[19] Scherman, Nosson, Meir Zlotowitz, Sheah Brander, and Menachem Davis. "Micah." In The Prophets: The Later Prophets with a Commentary Anthologized from the Rabbinic Writings. Brooklyn, NY: Mesorah Publications, 2013. p. 250.

5. What does it mean to strip the robe off a garment? (v. 8)

    Clothing was considered a valuable commodity in ancient days. It was not uncommon for people to be robbed as they traveled through the Promised Land. God is referring to this evil practice of stealing.

6. What does "I will speak out to you concerning wine and liquor" mean in verse 11?

    This verse in the Targum reads, "for they go astray after false prophets who prophesied to them by a spirit of deceit, and teach them about wine and drunkenness; and it shall be, as they are accustomed to go astray after false prophets, so the people of this generation shall be exiled to a land of falsehoods." Radak and Mahari Kara[20] believed that upon the receipt of drinks of wine as payment, the deceitful person would prophesy assurances of peace. Those who have already done the evil would preach peace because they have already gotten the gains they wanted.[21]

7. What does "the breaker go up before them" mean in verse 13?

    The Targum translates verse 13 as "the refugees shall go up as in the beginning, and a king shall go up leading at their head, and he shall destroy the enemy oppressing them and conquer the mighty citadels; they shall inherit the cities of the nations, and their kings shall eat at their head and the Memra of the Lord will be there support." The breaker refers to one who would breach a gate.

8. What does it mean that the king goes on before them and that the LORD is at their head in verse 13?

    The Messiah will break through all barriers that have been restraining Israel allowing their return to the Promised Land, according to the Sages. The Messiah will wage war

---

[20] **KARA, JOSEPH** (before c. 1060–70), Bible commentator from the north of France. The surname "Kara" (presumably Bible commentator) is an indication of Joseph's major occupation. The assumption that his surname means "teacher" is supported by his popular style and his frequent use of words in French (*la-az*), probably reflecting the fact that his commentaries are based on oral teaching. He wrote commentaries on most of the books of the Bible (possibly all), most of which remained in manuscript until recent times. Source: https://www.jewishvirtuallibrary.org/kara-joseph

[21] IBID. p. 255.

against Israel's enemies and capture many of their cities. Alternatively, the breaker is the prophet Elijah who will arrive prior to the final redemption to usher in the new age. Elijah will break through to the hearts of the people, persuading them to repent, and encouraging them to turn their hearts to God.[22]

Main/Center Point

The prophet Micah is warning the people that they have been performing evil acts in front of the Lord and they will reach a point where their evil can no longer be overlooked and the Lord will take action against them.

Scripture cross references

Verse 2	Jer 22:17; Amo 8:4; Isa 5:8; 1Ki 21:1-15
Verse 4	Hab 2:6; Jer 9:10, Jer 9:17-21; Mic 1:8; Isa 6:11; Isa 24:3; Jer 4:13; Jer 6:12; Jer 8:10
Verse 7	Hab 2:6; Jer 9:10; Jer 9:17-21; Isa 6:11; Isa 24:3; Jer 4:13; Jer 6:12; Jer 8:10
Verse 11	Jer 5:31; Isa 28:7; Isa 30:10; Isa 30:11

Culture Section

Discussion

Prior to World War I a person's property in the near East could be confiscated by kings, princes, and government officials. The poor were especially vulnerable to having their property confiscated in this way, enabling the royalty and the rich of the area to exploit them. The plans for confiscating property were done during the still hours of the night, when the wicked oppressors ate and drank, and then executed their plans during daylight. They would bring false charges against landowners in order to seize their

---

[22] IBID. p. 257.

property and would hire false witnesses to testify against them. Their trials were then held by judges who were friends of the rulers or by conspirators. Therefore Near Eastern rulers, princes, tax collectors, and richer oppressors were feared and hated by the people.[23]

Questioning the passage

1. What does it mean to walk after wind and falsehood? (v. 11)

    The word used for wind can also mean spirit. Just as men are moved by the spirit, false prophets were moved by the wind of falsehood. The reference here in verse 11 is to false prophets who predicted periods of prosperity, peace, and luxuries when there was no prosperity and war was at hand. It is easy to predict peace and prosperity, but difficult to warn people against impending calamities. Therefore true prophets were slain, but false prophets were often employed as royal counselors.

2. What is Micah saying about the remnant in verses 12 and 13?

    When the people returned home from the exile in Babylon, they had found that several Gentile nations had taken over their land. The breakers were people who knew how to establish a siege around the city with walls so that they could break through the walls and retake the city. Micah is giving us the hope of a restoration of the remnant, but that the remnant will have to fight to recover their land.

Zohar

The Zohar says that evil accumulates on the hands in the evening while we sleep. This idea could have developed out of verse 1 because it is through the power of our hands that evil is done.

---

[23] Errico, Rocco A., and George M. Lamsa. "Micah Chapter One." In Aramaic Light on Ezekiel, Daniel, and the Minor Prophets: A Commentary Based on the Aramaic Language and Ancient Near Eastern Customs. Smyrna, GA: Noohra Foundation, 2012., p. 170.

Thoughts

The social evil of stealing and confiscating property is spoken of in this chapter. The evil is planned in the evening and night when no one is aware of what is going on and is executed during the day. Micah also tells the people that it is too late to do anything about it. There comes a time when even the LORD is tired of all the evil that was going on and something had to be done about it. What is interesting is that the gathering of the remnant is spoken of before the destruction or exile has even occurred. This gives an interesting hope to the people that some of them will be saved, even though they do not know what is about to happen. It is interesting that the LORD would tell Micah to discuss the remnant before discussing the punishment. It also tells us that the Lord is forgiving, but there are certain points of evil where even God has to intervene. This chapter deals with the commandment that we find in the Ten Commandments about stealing.

Michael Harvey Koplitz

Micah Chapter 3

Language

New American Standard 1995	Hebrew	Septuagint
¹ And I said, "Hear now, heads of Jacob And rulers of the house of Israel. Is it not for you to know justice? ² "You who hate good and love evil, Who tear off their skin from them And their flesh from their bones, ³ Who eat the flesh of my people, Strip off their skin from them, Break their bones And chop *them* up as for the pot And as meat in a kettle." ⁴ Then they will cry out to the LORD, But He will not answer them. Instead, He will hide His face from them at that time Because they have practiced evil deeds. ⁵ Thus says the LORD concerning the prophets who lead my people astray; When they have *something* to bite with their teeth, They cry, "Peace," But against him who puts nothing in their mouths They declare holy war.	¹וָאֹמַר שִׁמְעוּ־נָא רָאשֵׁי יַעֲקֹב וּקְצִינֵי בֵּית יִשְׂרָאֵל הֲלוֹא לָכֶם לָדַעַת אֶת־הַמִּשְׁפָּט׃ ²שֹׂנְאֵי טוֹב וְאֹהֲבֵי (רָעָה) [רָע] גֹּזְלֵי עוֹרָם מֵעֲלֵיהֶם וּשְׁאֵרָם מֵעַל עַצְמוֹתָם׃ ³וַאֲשֶׁר אָכְלוּ שְׁאֵר עַמִּי וְעוֹרָם מֵעֲלֵיהֶם הִפְשִׁיטוּ וְאֶת־עַצְמֹתֵיהֶם פִּצֵּחוּ וּפָרְשׂוּ כַּאֲשֶׁר בַּסִּיר וּכְבָשָׂר בְּתוֹךְ קַלָּחַת׃ ⁴אָז יִזְעֲקוּ אֶל־יְהוָה וְלֹא יַעֲנֶה אוֹתָם וְיַסְתֵּר פָּנָיו מֵהֶם בָּעֵת הַהִיא כַּאֲשֶׁר הֵרֵעוּ מַעַלְלֵיהֶם׃ פ ⁵כֹּה אָמַר יְהוָה עַל־הַנְּבִיאִים הַמַּתְעִים אֶת־עַמִּי הַנֹּשְׁכִים בְּשִׁנֵּיהֶם וְקָרְאוּ שָׁלוֹם וַאֲשֶׁר לֹא־יִתֵּן עַל־פִּיהֶם וְקִדְּשׁוּ עָלָיו מִלְחָמָה׃ ⁶לָכֵן לַיְלָה לָכֶם מֵחָזוֹן וְחָשְׁכָה לָכֶם מִקְּסֹם וּבָאָה הַשֶּׁמֶשׁ עַל־הַנְּבִיאִים וְקָדַר עֲלֵיהֶם הַיּוֹם׃ ⁷וּבֹשׁוּ הַחֹזִים וְחָפְרוּ הַקֹּסְמִים וְעָטוּ עַל־שָׂפָם כֻּלָּם כִּי אֵין מַעֲנֵה אֱלֹהִים׃ ⁸וְאוּלָם אָנֹכִי מָלֵאתִי כֹחַ אֶת־רוּחַ יְהוָה וּמִשְׁפָּט וּגְבוּרָה לְהַגִּיד לְיַעֲקֹב פִּשְׁעוֹ וּלְיִשְׂרָאֵל חַטָּאתוֹ׃ ס ⁹שִׁמְעוּ־נָא זֹאת רָאשֵׁי בֵּית יַעֲקֹב וּקְצִינֵי בֵּית יִשְׂרָאֵל הַמְתַעֲבִים מִשְׁפָּט וְאֵת כָּל־הַיְשָׁרָה יְעַקֵּשׁוּ׃ ¹⁰בֹּנֶה צִיּוֹן בְּדָמִים וִירוּשָׁלִַם בְּעַוְלָה׃	¹ And he shall say, Hear now these words, ye heads of the house of Jacob, and ye remnant of the house of Israel; is it not for you to know judgment? ² *who* hate good, and seek evil; *who* tear their skins off them, and their flesh off their bones: ³ even as they devoured the flesh of my people, and stripped their skins off them, and broke their bones, and divided *them* as flesh for the caldron, and as meat for the pot, ⁴ thus they shall cry to the Lord, but he shall not hearken to them; and he shall turn away his face from them at that time, because they have done wickedly in their practices against themselves. ⁵ Thus saith the Lord concerning the prophets that lead my people astray, that bit with their teeth, and proclaim peace to them; and *when* nothing was put into their mouth,

⁶ Therefore *it will be* night for you-- without vision, And darkness for you-- without divination. The sun will go down on the prophets, And the day will become dark over them. ⁷ The seers will be ashamed And the diviners will be embarrassed. Indeed, they will all cover *their* mouths Because there is no answer from God. ⁸ On the other hand I am filled with power-- With the Spirit of the LORD-- And with justice and courage To make known to Jacob his rebellious act, Even to Israel his sin. ⁹ Now hear this, heads of the house of Jacob And rulers of the house of Israel, Who abhor justice And twist everything that is straight, ¹⁰ Who build Zion with bloodshed And Jerusalem with violent injustice. ¹¹ Her leaders pronounce judgment for a bribe, Her priests instruct for a price And her prophets divine for money. Yet they lean on the LORD saying, "Is not the LORD in our midst? Calamity will not come upon us." ¹² Therefore, on account of you Zion will be plowed as a field, Jerusalem will become a heap of ruins, And the mountain of the	¹¹ רָאשֶׁ֣יהָ ׀ בְּשֹׁ֣חַד יִשְׁפֹּ֗טוּ וְכֹהֲנֶ֙יהָ֙ בִּמְחִ֣יר יוֹר֔וּ וּנְבִיאֶ֖יהָ בְּכֶ֣סֶף יִקְסֹ֑מוּ וְעַל־יְהוָה֙ יִשָּׁעֵ֣נוּ לֵאמֹ֔ר הֲל֤וֹא יְהוָה֙ בְּקִרְבֵּ֔נוּ לֹֽא־תָב֥וֹא עָלֵ֖ינוּ רָעָֽה׃ ¹² לָכֵן֙ בִּגְלַלְכֶ֔ם צִיּ֖וֹן שָׂדֶ֣ה תֵֽחָרֵ֑שׁ וִירוּשָׁלִַ֙ם֙ עִיִּ֣ין תִּֽהְיֶ֔ה וְהַ֥ר הַבַּ֖יִת לְבָמ֥וֹת יָֽעַר׃ פ	they raised up war against them: ⁶ therefore there shall be night to you instead of a vision, and there shall be to you darkness instead of prophecy; and the sun shall go down upon the prophets, and the day shall be dark upon them. ⁷ And the seers of night-visions shall be ashamed, and the prophets shall be laughed to scorn: and all the people shall speak against them, because there shall be none to hearken to them. ⁸ Surely I will strengthen myself with the Spirit of the Lord, and of judgment, and of power, to declare to Jacob his transgressions, and to Israel his sins. ⁹ Hear now these words, ye chiefs of the house of Jacob, and the remnant of the house of Israel, who hate judgment, and pervert all righteousness; ¹⁰ who build up Sion with blood, and Jerusalem with iniquity. ¹¹ The heads thereof have judged for gifts, and the priests thereof have answered for hire, and her prophets have divined for silver: and *yet* they have rested on the Lord, saying, Is not the Lord among us? no evil shall come upon us.

temple *will become* high places of a forest.		[12] Therefore on your account Sion shall be ploughed as a field, and Jerusalem shall be as a storehouse of fruits, and the mountain of the house as a grove of the forest. (Mic. 3:1-12 LXA)

Process of Discovery
Linguistics Section

Linguistic Structure

> **A** [1] And I said, "Hear now, **heads of Jacob And rulers of the house of Israel**. Is it not for you to know justice? [2] "You who hate good and love evil, Who tear off their skin from them And their flesh from their bones, [3] Who eat the flesh of my people, Strip off their skin from them, Break their bones And chop *them* up as for the pot And as meat in a kettle."
>
>> **B** [4] Then they will cry out to the LORD, But **He will not answer them**. Instead, He will hide His face from them at that time Because they have practiced evil deeds.
>>
>>> **C** [5] Thus says the LORD concerning the prophets who lead my people astray; When they have *something* to bite with their teeth, They cry, "Peace," But against him who puts nothing in their mouths They declare holy war. [6] Therefore *it will be* night for you-- without vision, And darkness for you-- without divination. **The sun will go down on the prophets, And the day will become dark over them.**
>>
>> **B'** [7] The seers will be ashamed And the diviners will be embarrassed. Indeed, they will all cover *their* mouths Because **there is no answer from God.** [8] On the other hand I am filled with power-- With the Spirit of the LORD-- And with justice and courage To make known to Jacob his rebellious act, Even to Israel his sin.
>
> **A'** [9] Now hear this, **heads of the house of Jacob And rulers of the house of Israel,** Who abhor justice And twist everything that is straight, [10] Who build Zion with bloodshed And Jerusalem with violent injustice. [11] Her leaders pronounce judgment for a bribe, Her priests instruct for a price And her prophets divine for money. Yet they lean on the LORD saying, "Is not the LORD in our midst? Calamity will not come upon us." [12] Therefore, on account of you Zion will be plowed as a field, Jerusalem will become a heap of ruins, And the mountain of the temple *will become* high places of a forest.

Discussion

This chapter of Micah has a chiasm that draws our attention to the false prophets of the day. Verse six has to be examined to determine whether the time of the prophets refers to

God's prophets and the false prophets. Is the LORD saying He will not send anymore prophets because of the false prophets? There is one A-B-C-B'-A' chiasm.

Questioning the Passage

1. Why are the names Jacob and Israel used in verse 1?

    "The name Israel conveys a higher spiritual state than the name Jacob. Hence, the term "leaders of Jacob" is referring to the self-appointed leaders of the Ten Tribes, who had forcibly gained their positions of leadership. In contrast, "officers of the House of Israel" refer to the leaders of the kingdom of Judah, who were men of stature and royal ancestry and who were qualified for their positions of honor (Malbim)."[24]

2. Why are the leaders of Jacob being asked whether they "is it not for you to know justice? (v. 1)

    The leaders of Jacob, the Northern Kingdom, as stated in question #1, were not appointed by the LORD to lead the people. The leadership at the time of Micah got their power by force. Therefore, they did not have the approval of the LORD to execute justice, especially in the LORD's name.

3. What does it mean when the LORD covers His face? (v. 4)

    When the LORD covers His face, it means that His divine presence, the Shekinah, has left. Here the Shekinah left the Northern Kingdom. When the LORD covers His face, He is no longer seeing the troubles of the people nor their cries for justice. In addition, the LORD's protection of the Northern Kingdom was removed.

4. What does "the sun will go down on the prophets" mean? (v. 6)

    "The prophet is referring to the three categories of people who claimed to foretell the future: seers, diviners, and false prophets. Seers claimed to see their visions at night;

---

[24] Scherman, Nosson, Meir Zlotowitz, Sheah Brander, and Menachem Davis. "Micah." In The Prophets: The Later Prophets with a Commentary Anthologized from the Rabbinic Writings. Brooklyn, NY: Mesorah Publications, 2013. p. 257.

but instead of the night ushering in a vision, the vision will usher in the night. Diviners usually practiced their divinations in a dark place; instead of the darkness bringing divination, the divination will bring on the darkness. The false prophets prophesied by day. Their punishment was that the sun will set for them and their day will become dark (Malbim).[25]

Therefore, the day of the prophets is not ending at this point. Rather, the day of the false prophets of the Northern kingdom was about to end.

5. What does it mean to be plowed like a field? (v. 12)

   Micah is pronouncing destruction upon Jerusalem and the Temple. Being plowed like a field can mean that not only the buildings of the city will be destroyed, but also the foundations of the buildings will be destroyed.

Metaphors

1. What does the metaphor "tearing off their skin," "tearing flesh from their bones," and "eating the flesh of my people" mean? (v. 2)

   Verse two in the Targum speaks about the leadership who steals the property of the people. The tearing off of their skin and flesh refers to the people's belongings and their wealth.

Symbols

1. What is the symbolism of "the pot and kettle?" (v. 3)

   This is a repetition of the metaphor of "tearing skin and eating flesh." Micah is emphasizing how wrong it is for the leadership of God's people to rob God's people.

---

[25] IBID. p. 259

2. What is the symbolism of "something to bite with their teeth?" (v. 5)

    According to the Targum, people brought meat to the false prophets and for this gift, the false prophets gave these people false prophecies.

3. What is the symbolism of "covering the mouth?" (v. 7)

    Covering the mouth with a veil was done during mourning. "The false prophets will hide their faces in shame in the manner practiced by a mourner (Radak). Alternatively, the false prophets will actually mourn their fate when the terrible punishments occur (Metzudos)."[26]

4. What is the symbolism of a "high place of a forest?" (v. 12)

    After the Temple was destroyed by the Babylonians and the people removed from the city, there was no one left to maintain the remains of the Temple, therefore weeds and other plants could grow on the land. If Jerusalem was left alone for an elongated period it would have plant life growing on it and would resemble a forest, eventually.

Name of places

1. צִיּוֹן *Tsiyyon* **Meaning:** a mountain, also a name for Jerusalem
2. יְרוּשָׁלַם *Yerushalaim* or יְרוּשָׁלַיִם *Yerushalayim* **Meaning:** prob. 'foundation of peace,' capital city of all Israel

Scripture cross references

Verse 2	Psa 53:4; Eze 22:27
Verse 3	Psa 14:4; Psa 27:2; Zep 3:3; Eze 11:3, Eze 11:6, 7
Verse 6	Psa 14:4; Psa 27:2; Zep 3:3; Eze 11:3, Eze 11:6, 7

---

[26] Scherman, Nosson, Meir Zlotowitz, Sheah Brander, and Menachem Davis. "Micah." In The Prophets: The Later Prophets with a Commentary Anthologized from the Rabbinic Writings. Brooklyn, NY: Mesorah Publications, 2013. p. 257.

Main/Center Point

This chapter deals with what the LORD was going to do with the false prophets in Israel.

Culture Section

Discussion

The leaders of the people, judges and priests, did not receive payment for their work. Therefore, they would accept brides and would dispense justice based on bribes. These leaders would also invoke the name of God in their judgments even though God had nothing to do with the judgment. Micah is condemning this practice and tells us that these leaders will eventually be punished.

Thoughts

Micah attacks the practices of false prophets and the leaders of the people. Leaders have the responsibility to live by the Scriptures and to teach the people how to follow the Scriptures. In Micah's time the Priests and other leaders were using the Word of God for their own benefit and profit. By doing this they were leading the people astray and to sin. The difficulty of the time is that the people, mainly peasants, did not have the means to revolt against their leadership. Therefore, they continued to follow their leadership like sheep.

Micah Chapter Four

Language

New American Standard 1995	Hebrew	Septuagint
¹ And it will come about in the last days That the mountain of the house of the LORD Will be established as the chief of the mountains. It will be raised above the hills, And the peoples will stream to it. ² Many nations will come and say, "Come and let us go up to the mountain of the LORD And to the house of the God of Jacob, That He may teach us about His ways And that we may walk in His paths." For from Zion will go forth the law, Even the word of the LORD from Jerusalem. ³ And He will judge between many peoples And render decisions for mighty, distant nations. Then they will hammer their swords into plowshares And their spears into pruning hooks; Nation will not lift up sword against nation, And never again will they train for war. ⁴ Each of them will sit under his vine And under	¹ וְהָיָה ׀ בְּאַחֲרִית הַיָּמִים יִהְיֶה הַר בֵּית־יְהוָה נָכוֹן בְּרֹאשׁ הֶהָרִים וְנִשָּׂא הוּא מִגְּבָעוֹת וְנָהֲרוּ עָלָיו עַמִּים׃ ² וְהָלְכוּ גּוֹיִם רַבִּים וְאָמְרוּ לְכוּ ׀ וְנַעֲלֶה אֶל־הַר־יְהוָה וְאֶל־בֵּית אֱלֹהֵי יַעֲקֹב וְיוֹרֵנוּ מִדְּרָכָיו וְנֵלְכָה בְּאֹרְחֹתָיו כִּי מִצִּיּוֹן תֵּצֵא תוֹרָה וּדְבַר־יְהוָה מִירוּשָׁלִָם׃ ³ וְשָׁפַט בֵּין עַמִּים רַבִּים וְהוֹכִיחַ לְגוֹיִם עֲצֻמִים עַד־רָחוֹק וְכִתְּתוּ חַרְבֹתֵיהֶם לְאִתִּים וַחֲנִיתֹתֵיהֶם לְמַזְמֵרוֹת לֹא־יִשְׂאוּ גּוֹי אֶל־גּוֹי חֶרֶב וְלֹא־יִלְמְדוּן עוֹד מִלְחָמָה׃ ⁴ וְיָשְׁבוּ אִישׁ תַּחַת גַּפְנוֹ וְתַחַת תְּאֵנָתוֹ וְאֵין מַחֲרִיד כִּי־פִי יְהוָה צְבָאוֹת דִּבֵּר׃ ⁵ כִּי כָּל־הָעַמִּים יֵלְכוּ אִישׁ בְּשֵׁם אֱלֹהָיו וַאֲנַחְנוּ נֵלֵךְ בְּשֵׁם־יְהוָה אֱלֹהֵינוּ לְעוֹלָם וָעֶד׃ פ ⁶ בַּיּוֹם הַהוּא נְאֻם־יְהוָה אֹסְפָה הַצֹּלֵעָה וְהַנִּדָּחָה אֲקַבֵּצָה וַאֲשֶׁר הֲרֵעֹתִי׃ ⁷ וְשַׂמְתִּי אֶת־הַצֹּלֵעָה לִשְׁאֵרִית וְהַנַּהֲלָאָה לְגוֹי עָצוּם וּמָלַךְ יְהוָה עֲלֵיהֶם בְּהַר צִיּוֹן מֵעַתָּה וְעַד־עוֹלָם׃ פ ⁸ וְאַתָּה מִגְדַּל־עֵדֶר עֹפֶל בַּת־צִיּוֹן עָדֶיךָ תֵּאתֶה וּבָאָה הַמֶּמְשָׁלָה הָרִאשֹׁנָה מַמְלֶכֶת לְבַת־יְרוּשָׁלִָם׃ ⁹ עַתָּה לָמָּה תָרִיעִי רֵעַ הֲמֶלֶךְ אֵין־בָּךְ אִם־יוֹעֲצֵךְ אָבָד כִּי־הֶחֱזִיקֵךְ חִיל כַּיּוֹלֵדָה׃ ¹⁰ חוּלִי וָגֹחִי בַּת־צִיּוֹן כַּיּוֹלֵדָה כִּי־עַתָּה תֵצְאִי מִקִּרְיָה וְשָׁכַנְתְּ בַּשָּׂדֶה וּבָאת עַד־בָּבֶל שָׁם	¹ And at the last days the mountain of the Lord shall be manifest, established on the tops of the mountains, and it shall be exalted above the hills; and the peoples shall hasten to it. ² And many nations shall go, and say, Come, let us go up to the mountain of the Lord, and to the house of the God of Jacob; and they shall shew us his way, and we will walk in his paths: for out of Sion shall go forth a law, and the word of the Lord from Jerusalem. ³ And he shall judge among many peoples, and shall rebuke strong nations afar off; and they shall beat their swords into ploughshares, and their spears into sickles; and nation shall no more lift up sword against nation, neither shall they learn to war any more. ⁴ And every one shall rest under his vine, and every one under his fig-tree; and there shall be none to alarm *them*: for the mouth of the Lord Almighty has spoken these *words*.

49

his fig tree, With no one to make *them* afraid, For the mouth of the LORD of hosts has spoken.

⁵ Though all the peoples walk Each in the name of his god, As for us, we will walk In the name of the LORD our God forever and ever.

⁶ "In that day," declares the LORD, "I will assemble the lame And gather the outcasts, Even those whom I have afflicted.

⁷ "I will make the lame a remnant And the outcasts a strong nation, And the LORD will reign over them in Mount Zion From now on and forever.

⁸ "As for you, tower of the flock, Hill of the daughter of Zion, To you it will come-- Even the former dominion will come, The kingdom of the daughter of Jerusalem.

⁹ "Now, why do you cry out loudly? Is there no king among you, Or has your counselor perished, That agony has gripped you like a woman in childbirth?

¹⁰ "Writhe and labor to give birth, Daughter of Zion, Like a woman in childbirth; For now you will go out of the city, Dwell in the field, And go to Babylon. There you will be rescued; There the

תִּנָּצֵ֔לִי שָׁ֥ם יִגְאָלֵ֖ךְ יְהוָ֥ה מִכַּ֥ף אֹיְבָֽיִךְ׃
¹¹ וְעַתָּ֛ה נֶאֶסְפ֥וּ עָלַ֖יִךְ גּוֹיִ֣ם רַבִּ֑ים הָאֹמְרִ֣ים תֶּחֱנָ֔ף וְתַ֥חַז בְּצִיּ֖וֹן עֵינֵֽינוּ׃
¹² וְהֵ֗מָּה לֹ֤א יָֽדְעוּ֙ מַחְשְׁב֣וֹת יְהוָ֔ה וְלֹ֥א הֵבִ֖ינוּ עֲצָת֑וֹ כִּ֥י קִבְּצָ֖ם כֶּעָמִ֥יר גֹּֽרְנָה׃
¹³ ק֧וּמִי וָד֣וֹשִׁי בַת־צִיּ֗וֹן כִּֽי־קַרְנֵ֞ךְ אָשִׂ֤ים בַּרְזֶל֙ וּפַרְסֹתַ֣יִךְ אָשִׂ֣ים נְחוּשָׁ֔ה וַהֲדִקּ֖וֹת עַמִּ֣ים רַבִּ֑ים וְהַחֲרַמְתִּ֤י לַֽיהוָה֙ בִּצְעָ֔ם וְחֵילָ֖ם לַאֲד֥וֹן כָּל־הָאָֽרֶץ׃
¹⁴ עַתָּה֙ תִּתְגֹּדְדִ֣י בַת־גְּד֔וּד מָצ֖וֹר שָׂ֣ם עָלֵ֑ינוּ בַּשֵּׁ֙בֶט֙ יַכּ֣וּ עַֽל־הַלְּחִ֔י אֵ֖ת שֹׁפֵ֥ט יִשְׂרָאֵֽל׃ ס

⁵ For all *other* nations shall walk everyone in his own way, but we will walk in the name of the Lord our God for ever and ever.

⁶ In that day, saith the Lord, I will gather her that is bruised, and will receive her that is cast out, and those whom I rejected.

⁷ And I will make her that was bruised a remnant, and her that was rejected a mighty nation: and the Lord shall reign over them in mount Sion from henceforth, even for ever.

⁸ And thou, dark tower of the flock, daughter of Sion, on thee the dominion shall come and enter in, *even* the first kingdom from Babylon to the daughter of Jerusalem.

⁹ And now, why hast thou known calamities? was there not a king to thee? or has thy counsel perished that pangs as of a woman in travail have seized upon thee?

¹⁰ Be in pain, and strengthen thyself, and draw near, O daughter of Sion, as a woman in travail: for now thou shalt go forth out of the city, and shalt lodge in the plain, and shalt reach even to Babylon: thence shall the Lord thy God deliver thee, and thence shall he redeem

LORD will redeem you From the hand of your enemies. ¹¹ "And now many nations have been assembled against you Who say, 'Let her be polluted, And let our eyes gloat over Zion.' ¹² "But they do not know the thoughts of the LORD, And they do not understand His purpose; For He has gathered them like sheaves to the threshing floor. ¹³ "Arise and thresh, daughter of Zion, For your horn I will make iron And your hoofs I will make bronze, That you may pulverize many peoples, That you may devote to the LORD their unjust gain And their wealth to the Lord of all the earth.		thee out of the hand of thine enemies. ¹¹ And now have many nations gathered against thee, saying, We will rejoice, and our eyes shall look upon Sion. ¹² But they know not the thought of the Lord, and have not understood his counsel: for he has gathered them as sheaves of the floor. ¹³ Arise, and thresh them, O daughter of Sion: for I will make thine horns iron, and I will make thine hoofs brass: and thou shalt utterly destroy many nations, and shalt consecrate their abundance to the Lord, and their strength to the Lord of all the earth.

Process of Discovery
Linguistics Section

Linguistic Structure

A ¹ And it will come about **in the last days** That the mountain of the house of the LORD Will be established as the chief of the mountains. It will be raised above the hills, And the peoples will stream to it. ² Many nations will come and say, "Come and let us go up to the mountain of the LORD And to the house of the God of Jacob, That He may teach us about His ways And that we may walk in His paths." For from Zion will go forth the law, Even the word of the LORD from Jerusalem.

B ³ And He will judge between many peoples And render decisions for mighty, **distant nations.** Then they will hammer their swords into plowshares And their spears into pruning hooks; Nation will not lift up sword against nation, And never again will they train for war. ⁴ Each of them will sit under his vine And under his fig tree, With no one to make *them* afraid, For the mouth of the LORD of hosts has spoken. ⁵ Though all the peoples walk Each in the name of his god, As for us, we will walk In the name of the LORD our God forever and ever.

A' [6] **"In that day,"** declares the LORD, "I will assemble the lame And gather the outcasts, Even those whom I have afflicted.

B' [7] "I will make the lame a remnant And the **outcasts a strong nation**, And the LORD will reign over them in Mount Zion From now on and forever.

S [8] "As for you, tower of the flock, Hill of the **daughter of Zion**, To you it will come-- Even the former dominion will come, The kingdom of the daughter of Jerusalem. [9] "Now, why do you cry out loudly? Is there no king among you, Or has your counselor perished, That agony has gripped you like a woman in childbirth?

S1 [10] "Writhe and labor to give birth, **Daughter of Zion**, Like a woman in childbirth; For now you will go out of the city, Dwell in the field, And go to Babylon. There you will be rescued; There the LORD will redeem you From the hand of your enemies. [11] "And now many nations have been assembled against you Who say, 'Let her be polluted, And let our eyes gloat over Zion.' [12] "But they do not know the thoughts of the LORD, And they do not understand His purpose; For He has gathered them like sheaves to the threshing floor.

S2 [13] "Arise and thresh, **daughter of Zion**, For your horn I will make iron And your hoofs I will make bronze, That you may pulverize many peoples, That you may devote to the LORD their unjust gain And their wealth to the Lord of all the earth.

Discussion

This chapter consists of an A-B-A'-B' chiasm followed by three statements about the daughters of Zion (the inhabitants of the city).

Questioning the Passage

1. When will the last days come? (v. 1)

    The last days refer to the Messianic age (Radak). When this occurs the evil doers of the world will be destroyed. The last days can also be viewed as the end of history and the end of the Earth.[27] There is no indication as to when the Last Days will come.

---

[27] Scherman, Nosson, Meir Zlotowitz, Sheah Brander, and Menachem Davis. "Micah." In The Prophets: The Later Prophets with a Commentary Anthologized from the Rabbinic Writings. Brooklyn, NY: Mesorah Publications, 2013. p. 261.

2. Where is the mountain of the LORD? (v. 1)

    The mountain of the LORD is Mount Zion. On the top of Mount Zion is the city of Jerusalem. In Micah's day, the Temple of the LORD was a part of the city of Jerusalem.

3. What does it mean to be the chief mountain? (v. 1)

    The chief mountain means that Mount Zion will be established as the most prominent mountain in the world because it is where the sanctuary of the LORD lives.

4. What does it mean "to hammer their swords into plowshares" and "their spears into pruning hooks"? (v. 3)

    There will no longer be a need to have weapons of war in the Messianic age. Therefore, the people will take their weapons of war and will transform them into farming implements. Since the economy was agricultural, it makes sense that the people would want to use the metals of the weapons of war as plowshares.

5. What does the phrase "tower of the flock" mean? (v. 8)

    The Targum says that Mount Zion will be hidden when the LORD pronounces and then executes judgment upon the people for their sins. However, a remnant of the people will be restored by the LORD and the kingdom will be restored at Jerusalem. The Tower of the Flock, according to the Targum Yonasan. Radak believed that the Tower of the Flock is the Tower of David, which is the Temple of the LORD. It was a shepherd's watchtower near Bethlehem. Benjamin was born in Bethlehem which completed the twelve tribes. Thus, if Micah is discussing the Messiah being born in Bethlehem, he is referring to the birth of Yeshua.[28]

---

[28] IBID. p. 263.

An opinion is that Israel was a complete nation when Benjamin was born. This is confirmed in the Zohar and other sacred writings. When the Assyrians destroyed the Northern Kingdom and the Ten Tribes, Israel was then incomplete. The Messiah will usher in the Messianic age. When the Word of Yeshua is spread around the world and all come to believe in Him, Israel will be complete. Yeshua grafts the Gentiles in as the "Ten Tribes." Since the people who made up the ten tribes were scattered into the Assyrian Empire, some of their essence exists in all Gentiles. The Messianic Age will see the completion of Israel again when all evil and sin are removed from the Earth. Evil people will be destroyed and the remaining Gentiles will be a part of Israel, thus making Israel complete.

6. What does "hill of the daughter of Zion" mean? (v. 8)

    "Like migdal, ophel is a tower or fortress (Metzudos). The remnant of the lame and the weak will come back to you – the migdal [the Messianic king, the Temple, or Jerusalem] (Rashi). Alternately, Targum Yonasan interprets the verse as if the word ophel were written with an aleph, darkness, and translates 'the Messiah of Israel who had been concealed [who was held in darkness] due to the sins of those who assembled in Zion.'"[29]

7. Why are the people crying in verse 9?

    When the people cry out, it is because they are crying out to the LORD for His protection, which they lost because of their sins. Now they want the LORD's protection.

---

[29] IBID. p. 265

8. What is the symbolism of a woman in labor? (v. 10)

   The pain that a woman experiences during childbirth is one of the worst pains she has to endure. The punishment the LORD was going to bring upon Israel was going to be that painful.

Metaphors

1. Threshing floor in verse 12.

   "Arise and thresh" means to cut one's enemies into pieces and destroy them. In the Middle East, grains were threshed under the feet of oxen and threshing instruments that had teeth of iron. "Iron horns and bronze hoofs" refer to great strength and endurance.[30]

Symbols

1. The mountain of the LORD in verse 1

   The mountain in this verse is symbolic of the nation of Israel. Micah foresees salvation to the remnant of the Hebrew people. This is a verse of hope that the mighty city of God, Jerusalem, and the Temple will be rebuilt. The fortunes of Israel will one day return. In the Messianic kingdom, pagan images and practices will be destroyed and God's reign of peace and harmony will be triumphant.[31]

Name of places

1. צִיּוֹן *Tsiyyon* (851b) **Meaning:** a mountain in Jerusalem, also a name for Jerusalem

---

[30] Errico, Rocco A., and George M. Lamsa. "Micah Chapter Four." In Aramaic Light on Ezekiel, Daniel, and the Minor Prophets: A Commentary Based on the Aramaic Language and Ancient Near Eastern Customs. Smyma, GA: Noohra Foundation, 2012.

[31] Errico, Rocco A., and George M. Lamsa. "Micah Chapter Four." In Aramaic Light on Ezekiel, Daniel, and the Minor Prophets: A Commentary Based on the Aramaic Language and Ancient Near Eastern Customs. Smyma, GA: Noohra Foundation, 2012.

Scripture cross references

Verse 1	Isa 2:2-4; Dan 2:28; Dan 10:14; Hos 3:5; Eze 43:12; Zec 8:3; Psa 22:27; Psa 86:9; Jer 3:17
Verse 5	2Ki 17:29; Zec 10:12; Jos 24:15; Isa 26:8, Isa 26:13
Verse 6	Zep 3:19; Psa 147:2; Eze 34:13, Eze 34:16; Eze 37:21
Verse 7	Isa 24:23
Verse 8	Psa 48:3, Psa 48:12; Psa 61:3; Isa 1:26; Zec 9:10
Verse 9	Jer 8:19; Isa 3:1-3
Verse 10	Mic 5:3; 2Ki 20:18; Hos 2:14; Isa 43:14; Isa 45:13; Mic 7:8-12; Isa 48:20; Isa 52:9-12
Verse 11	Isa 5:25-30; Isa 17:12-14
Verse 12	Psa 147:19, Psa 147:20

Main/Center Point

Micah offers the light of hope that a remnant of the people will survive the Exile and will be able to return to the land and rebuild God's city and His Temple.

Culture Section

Discussion
N/A

Questioning the passage

1. What does the verse 3 reference to hammer, swords, etc., mean?

    "The reference is to the coming of the Messiah, the great Deliverer of Israel. All human efforts had failed to assure Israel's sovereignty."[32] Until this time Israel was only confronted by the smaller and weaker nations around her borders. Now a huge

---
[32] IBID.

power was knocking at the door. The Assyrians could not be dealt with like the Canaanites or Amalekites. When the Messiah came, all the Gentile nations were to be defeated and all the people of Israel would be gathered together in the Promised Land. This prophecy of Micah gave hope to the people of Judah, who saw their brethren of the Northern Kingdom being destroyed.

2. Sitting under fig trees in verse 4.

    This means that people will be without fear and tranquility will be in the land. Vines are planted in the Middle East to offer shade from the sun of the summer months. Families would sit together under the plants in the shade. When the Kingdom of God comes, the people sitting under the fig trees will not be disturbed.[33]

3. Verse 11-13 tell us what?

    When Israel is restored by the remnant of the people, they would face considerable opposition from the nations who occupied their land during the Babylonian Exile. They would have to fight off the occupiers who did not give back the land so quickly.

Thoughts

This chapter is where Micah tells the people of Jerusalem that there is hope that God will restore a remnant of the people to the city. The people are told that one day the city of Jerusalem and the Temple would be rebuilt. Even though these words of hope are good to have, the horror of the destruction of God's city and Temple will have to precede the rebuild. Had the people listened to all the prophets the LORD sent, there would be no need for punishment.

---

[33] IBID.

Micah Chapter Five

Language

New American Standard 1995	Hebrew	Septuagint
[1] "Now muster yourselves in troops, daughter of troops; They have laid siege against us; With a rod they will smite the judge of Israel on the cheek. [2] "But as for you, Bethlehem Ephrathah, *Too* little to be among the clans of Judah, From you One will go forth for Me to be ruler in Israel. His goings forth are from long ago, From the days of eternity." [3] Therefore He will give them *up* until the time When she who is in labor has borne a child. Then the remainder of His brethren Will return to the sons of Israel. [4] And He will arise and shepherd *His flock* In the strength of the LORD, In the majesty of the name of the LORD His God. And they will remain, Because at that time He will be great To the ends of the earth. [5] This One will be *our* peace. When the Assyrian invades our land, When he tramples on our citadels,	[1] וְאַתָּה בֵּית־לֶחֶם אֶפְרָתָה צָעִיר לִהְיוֹת בְּאַלְפֵי יְהוּדָה מִמְּךָ לִי יֵצֵא לִהְיוֹת מוֹשֵׁל בְּיִשְׂרָאֵל וּמוֹצָאֹתָיו מִקֶּדֶם מִימֵי עוֹלָם׃ [2] לָכֵן יִתְּנֵם עַד־עֵת יוֹלֵדָה יָלָדָה וְיֶתֶר אֶחָיו יְשׁוּבוּן עַל־בְּנֵי יִשְׂרָאֵל׃ [3] וְעָמַד וְרָעָה בְּעֹז יְהוָה בִּגְאוֹן שֵׁם יְהוָה אֱלֹהָיו וְיָשָׁבוּ כִּי־עַתָּה יִגְדַּל עַד־אַפְסֵי־אָרֶץ׃ [4] וְהָיָה זֶה שָׁלוֹם אַשּׁוּר כִּי־יָבוֹא בְאַרְצֵנוּ וְכִי יִדְרֹךְ בְּאַרְמְנֹתֵינוּ וַהֲקֵמֹנוּ עָלָיו שִׁבְעָה רֹעִים וּשְׁמֹנָה נְסִיכֵי אָדָם׃ [5] וְרָעוּ אֶת־אֶרֶץ אַשּׁוּר בַּחֶרֶב וְאֶת־אֶרֶץ נִמְרֹד בִּפְתָחֶיהָ וְהִצִּיל מֵאַשּׁוּר כִּי־יָבוֹא בְאַרְצֵנוּ וְכִי יִדְרֹךְ בִּגְבוּלֵנוּ׃ ס [6] וְהָיָה שְׁאֵרִית יַעֲקֹב בְּקֶרֶב עַמִּים רַבִּים כְּטַל מֵאֵת יְהוָה כִּרְבִיבִים עֲלֵי־עֵשֶׂב אֲשֶׁר לֹא־יְקַוֶּה לְאִישׁ וְלֹא יְיַחֵל לִבְנֵי אָדָם׃ [7] וְהָיָה שְׁאֵרִית יַעֲקֹב בַּגּוֹיִם בְּקֶרֶב עַמִּים רַבִּים כְּאַרְיֵה בְּבַהֲמוֹת יַעַר כִּכְפִיר בְּעֶדְרֵי צֹאן אֲשֶׁר אִם עָבַר וְרָמַס וְטָרַף וְאֵין מַצִּיל׃ [8] תָּרֹם יָדְךָ עַל־צָרֶיךָ וְכָל־אֹיְבֶיךָ יִכָּרֵתוּ׃ פ [9] וְהָיָה בַיּוֹם־הַהוּא נְאֻם־יְהוָה וְהִכְרַתִּי סוּסֶיךָ מִקִּרְבֶּךָ וְהַאֲבַדְתִּי מַרְכְּבֹתֶיךָ׃	Now shall the daughter *of Sion* be completely hedged in: he has laid siege against us: they shall smite the tribes of Israel with a rod upon the cheek. [2] And thou, Bethleem, house of Ephratha, art few in number to be *reckoned* among the thousands of Juda; *yet* out of thee shall one come forth to me, to be a ruler of Israel; and his goings forth were from the beginning, *even* from eternity. [3] Therefore shall he appoint them *to wait* till the time of her that travails: she shall bring forth, and *then* the remnant of their brethren shall return to the children of Israel. [4] And the Lord shall stand, and see, and feed his flock with power, and they shall dwell in the glory of the name of the Lord their God: for now shall they be magnified to the ends of the earth. [5] And she shall have peace when Assur shall come into your land, and when he shall come up upon

Then we will raise against him Seven shepherds and eight leaders of men. ⁶ They will shepherd the land of Assyria with the sword, The land of Nimrod at its entrances; And He will deliver *us* from the Assyrian When he attacks our land And when he tramples our territory. ⁷ Then the remnant of Jacob Will be among many peoples Like dew from the LORD, Like showers on vegetation Which do not wait for man Or delay for the sons of men. ⁸ The remnant of Jacob Will be among the nations, Among many peoples Like a lion among the beasts of the forest, Like a young lion among flocks of sheep, Which, if he passes through, Tramples down and tears, And there is none to rescue. ⁹ Your hand will be lifted up against your adversaries, And all your enemies will be cut off. ¹⁰ "It will be in that day," declares the LORD, "That I will cut off your horses from among you And destroy your chariots. ¹¹ "I will also cut off the cities of your land And tear down all your fortifications.	¹⁰ וְהִכְרַתִּ֛י עָרֵ֥י אַרְצֶ֖ךָ וְהָרַסְתִּ֥י כָּל־מִבְצָרֶֽיךָ׃ ¹¹ וְהִכְרַתִּ֥י כְשָׁפִ֖ים מִיָּדֶ֑ךָ וּֽמְעוֹנְנִ֖ים לֹ֥א יִֽהְיוּ־לָֽךְ׃ ¹² וְהִכְרַתִּ֧י פְסִילֶ֛יךָ וּמַצֵּבוֹתֶ֖יךָ מִקִּרְבֶּ֑ךָ וְלֹֽא־תִשְׁתַּחֲוֶ֥ה ע֖וֹד לְמַעֲשֵׂ֥ה יָדֶֽיךָ׃ ¹³ וְנָתַשְׁתִּ֥י אֲשֵׁירֶ֖יךָ מִקִּרְבֶּ֑ךָ וְהִשְׁמַדְתִּ֖י עָרֶֽיךָ׃ ¹⁴ וְעָשִׂ֜יתִי בְּאַ֤ף וּבְחֵמָה֙ נָקָ֔ם אֶת־הַגּוֹיִ֖ם אֲשֶׁ֥ר לֹ֥א שָׁמֵֽעוּ׃ ס	your country; and there shall be raised up against him seven shepherds, and eight attacks of men. ⁶ And they shall tend the Assyrian with a sword, and the land of Nebrod with her trench: and he shall deliver *you* from the Assyrian, when he shall come upon your land, and when he shall invade your coasts. ⁷ And the remnant of Jacob shall be among the Gentiles in the midst of many peoples, as dew falling from the Lord, and as lambs on the grass; that none may assemble nor resist among the sons of men. ⁸ And the remnant of Jacob shall be among the Gentiles in the midst of many nations, as a lion in the forest among cattle, and as a *lion's* whelp among the flocks of sheep, even as when he goes through, and selects, and carries off *his prey*, and there is none to deliver. ⁹ Thine hand shall be lifted up against them that afflict thee, and all thine enemies shall be utterly destroyed. ¹⁰ And it shall come to pass in that day, saith the Lord, *that* I will utterly destroy the horses out of the midst of thee, and destroy thy chariots;

¹² "I will cut off sorceries from your hand, And you will have fortune-tellers no more. ¹³ "I will cut off your carved images And your *sacred* pillars from among you, So that you will no longer bow down To the work of your hands. ¹⁴ "I will root out your Asherim from among you And destroy your cities. ¹⁵ "And I will execute vengeance in anger and wrath On the nations which have not obeyed."		¹¹ and I will utterly destroy the cities of thy land, and demolish all thy strongholds: ¹² and I will utterly destroy thy sorceries out of thine hands; and there shall be no soothsayers in thee. ¹³ And I will utterly destroy thy graven images, and thy statues out of the midst of thee; and thou shalt never any more worship the works of thine hands. ¹⁴ And I will cut off the groves out of the midst of thee, and I will abolish thy cities. ¹⁵ and I will execute vengeance on the heathen in anger and wrath, because they hearkened not.

Process of Discovery
   Linguistics Section

   Linguistic Structure

> **A** ¹ "Now muster yourselves in troops, daughter of troops; They have laid siege against us; With a rod they will smite the judge of Israel on the cheek. ² "But as for you, Bethlehem Ephrathah, *Too* little to be among the clans of Judah, From you One will go forth for Me to be ruler in Israel. His goings forth are from long ago, From the days of eternity." ³ Therefore He will give them *up* until the time When she who is in labor has borne a child. **Then the remainder of His brethren Will return to the sons of Israel.** ⁴ And He will arise and shepherd *His flock* In the strength of the LORD, In the majesty of the name of the LORD His God. And they will remain, Because at that time He will be great To the ends of the earth.
>
>> **B** ⁵ This One will be *our* peace. When the Assyrian invades our land, When he tramples on our citadels, Then we will raise against him Seven shepherds and eight leaders of men. ⁶ They will shepherd the land of Assyria with the sword, The land of Nimrod at its entrances; And He will deliver *us* from the Assyrian When he attacks our land And when he tramples our territory.
>
> **A'** ⁷ Then the **remnant of Jacob** Will be among many peoples Like dew from the LORD, Like showers on vegetation Which do not wait for man Or delay for the sons of men. ⁸ The remnant of Jacob Will be among the nations, Among many peoples Like a lion among the beasts of the forest, Like a young lion among flocks of sheep, Which, if he passes through, Tramples down and tears, And there is none to rescue.
>
>> **B'** ⁹ Your hand will be lifted up against your adversaries, And all your enemies will be cut off.
>
> **A** ¹⁰ "It will be in that day," declares the LORD, "That I will cut off your horses from among you And destroy your chariots.
>
> **A1** ¹¹ "I will also cut off the cities of your land And tear down all your fortifications.
>
> **A2** ¹² "I will cut off sorceries from your hand, And you will have fortune-tellers no more.
>
> **A4** ¹³ "I will cut off your carved images And your *sacred* pillars from among you, So that you will no longer bow down To the work of your hands.
>
> **A5** ¹⁴ "I will root out your Asherim from among you And destroy your cities.

A6 [15] "And I will execute vengeance in anger and wrath On the nations which have not obeyed."

Discussion

The chapter consists of a simple A-B-A'-B' chiasm and then seven statements.

Questioning the Passage

1. Who are the "daughters of troops?" (v. 1)

    One thought about this verse is that when the invasion and siege of Judah occurs, even the women will have to join the fight.

2. Who is the judge of Israel? (v. 1)

    What this phrase is referring to has to include the words "on the cheek." The reference is that Israel had struck its prophets and judges on the cheek. They were guilty of disgracing and humiliating them. The reference tells us that in the Messianic times, Israel will be punished for the disgrace of its judges during the Exile period (Metzudos).[34]

3. Why is Bethlehem Ephratha called out in verse 2?

    Bethlehem was the birthplace of King David. Since the LORD promised King David that an ancestor of his line would sit on the throne, the prophet reminds us that the LORD will eventually (and did) raise a new Davidic monarch and will inaugurate an age of security for Israel.[35]

---

[34] Scherman, Nosson, Meir Zlotowitz, Sheah Brander, and Menachem Davis. "Micah." In The Prophets: The Later Prophets with a Commentary Anthologized from the Rabbinic Writings. Brooklyn, NY: Mesorah Publications, 2013. p. 269.
[35] Sweeney, Marvin Alan, David W. Cotter, Chris Franke, and Jerome T. Walsh. "Micah." In *Micah, Nahum, Habakkuk, Zephaniah, Haggai, Zechariah, Malachi*. Collegeville, MN: Liturgical Press, 2000.

4. What is the meaning of the sign offered in verse 3?

    When a woman is in labor, she suffers severe pain. The prophecy says that the people left in the city of Jerusalem will suffer similar pain when the siege of the city occurred.

5. Who are the seven shepherds and eight leaders in verse 5?

    Radak wrote that the seven shepherds and eight leaders will assist the Messianic King in leading Israel. Radak explained the numbers are uneven, which can be found in Ecclesiastes (11:2) where a similar phrase is used. The seven shepherds are: David in the center; Adam, Seth, and Methuselah on his right; Abraham, Jacob and Moses on his left. The eight officers will be Jesse, Saul, Samuel, Amos, Zephaniah, Hezekiah, Elijah and the Messiah.[36]

6. Where was the land of Nimrod? (v. 6)

    The reference to the land of Nimrod recalls the ancient Mesopotamian king and cultural hero who established the Assyrian cities of Nineveh and Calah as well as the cities of Babylon, Erech and Accad.[37] The land of Nimrod would be Iraq today.

7. What does the simile "like dew from the LORD" mean? (v. 7)

    This simile means that humans cannot control the rain or dew, only the LORD can do this. Israel will turn to the LORD for help when the invasion had begun.[38]

8. What does the simile "like showers on vegetation" mean? (v. 7)

    This simile means the same thing as the simile "like dew from the LORD."

---

[36] Scherman, Nosson, Meir Zlotowitz, Sheah Brander, and Menachem Davis. "Micah." In The Prophets: The Later Prophets with a Commentary Anthologized from the Rabbinic Writings. Brooklyn, NY: Mesorah Publications, 2013. p. 271.
[37] Sweeney, Marvin Alan, David W. Cotter, Chris Franke, and Jerome T. Walsh. "Micah." In *Micah, Nahum, Habakkuk, Zephaniah, Haggai, Zechariah, Malachi*. Collegeville, MN: Liturgical Press, 2000.
[38] Scherman, Nosson, Meir Zlotowitz, Sheah Brander, and Menachem Davis. "Micah." In The Prophets: The Later Prophets with a Commentary Anthologized from the Rabbinic Writings. Brooklyn, NY: Mesorah Publications, 2013. p. 271.

9. What day is the LORD speaking of in verse 10?

    This day is when the war of Gog and Magog is over. It should be noted that the prophet is discussing the battles at the End of Times.[39] When this happens, Israel will never need horses or chariots because God will protect them and no enemy will ever revolt against Israel again. This connects to verse nine where the LORD raises His hand and destroys all of Israel's enemies.

Symbols

1. "Your hand will be lifted up…" (v. 9)

    When the hand of the LORD is lifted up it symbolizes victory.

Name of places

1. בֵּית לֶחֶם *Beth Lechem* **Meaning:** 'place of bread,' a city in Judah, also a city in Zebulun, Bethlehem

Scripture cross references

Verse 3	Hos 11:8; Isa 10:20-22
Verse 4	Isa 40:11; Isa 49:9; Eze 34:13-15, Eze 34:23, 24; Isa 45:22; Isa 52:10
Verse 5	Isa 9:6; Luk 2:14; Eph 2:14; Col 1:20, Isa 8:7, Isa 8:8; Isa 10:24-27
Verse 6	Gen 49:9; Num 24:9, Psa 44:5; Isa 41:15, Isa 41:16; Zec 10:5, Hos 5:14, Psa 50:22
Verse 7	Deu 32:2; Psa 110:3; Hos 14:5; Psa 72:6; Isa 44:3
Verse 8	Gen 49:9; Num 24:9; Psa 44:5; Isa 41:15, Isa 41:16; Mic 4:13; Zec 10:5; Hos 5:14; Psa 50:22
Verse 12	Deu 18:10-12; Isa 2:6; Isa 8:19
Verse 13	Isa 2:18; Isa 17:8; Eze 6:9

---

[39] IBID.

Verse 15   Isa 1:24; Isa 65:12

Main/Center Point

This chapter is referencing about the end of time. The prophecy is that the LORD will come to Earth and battle the enemies of Israel. The enemies of Israel are the enemies of the LORD. When the battles of Gog and Magog are complete the LORD will be victorious because He will lift His hand in victory. The need for armies and weapons of war will be done. The LORD will restore the nation of Israel as it should be. No longer will Israel stray away from the worship of the LORD because all the things that cause Israel to stray will be destroyed.

Thoughts

The remnant of Israel will be returned to the Promised Land at the end of time after the battle of Gog and Magog. The Messiah will be sent from the LORD and the Messianic age will begin. The Messiah will be a descendant of David and with the help of fifteen men of Israel's past, the land will be secured and the enemies of the LORD, which are also the enemies of Israel, will perish. Once the Messianic age begins all the weapons that man has developed for war will be destroyed by the LORD because they will no longer be needed. The idols and other materials that assisted in Israel's defection from the worship of the LORD will be destroyed. None of these things will be necessary in the Messianic age.

Understanding Micah

Micah Chapter Six

Language

New Standard American 1995	Hebrew	Septuagint
¹ Hear now what the LORD is saying, "Arise, plead your case before the mountains, And let the hills hear your voice. ² "Listen, you mountains, to the indictment of the LORD, And you enduring foundations of the earth, Because the LORD has a case against His people; Even with Israel He will dispute. ³ "My people, what have I done to you, And how have I wearied you? Answer Me. ⁴ "Indeed, I brought you up from the land of Egypt And ransomed you from the house of slavery, And I sent before you Moses, Aaron and Miriam. ⁵ "My people, remember now What Balak king of Moab counseled And what Balaam son of Beor answered him, *And* from Shittim to Gilgal, So that you might know the righteous acts of the LORD." ⁶ With what shall I come to the LORD *And* bow myself before the God on high? Shall I come to Him	¹ שִׁמְעוּ־נָא אֵת אֲשֶׁר־יְהוָה אֹמֵר קוּם רִיב אֶת־הֶהָרִים וְתִשְׁמַעְנָה הַגְּבָעוֹת קוֹלֶךָ׃ ² שִׁמְעוּ הָרִים אֶת־רִיב יְהוָה וְהָאֵתָנִים מֹסְדֵי אָרֶץ כִּי רִיב לַיהוָה עִם־עַמּוֹ וְעִם־יִשְׂרָאֵל יִתְוַכָּח׃ ³ עַמִּי מֶה־עָשִׂיתִי לְךָ וּמָה הֶלְאֵתִיךָ עֲנֵה בִּי׃ ⁴ כִּי הֶעֱלִתִיךָ מֵאֶרֶץ מִצְרַיִם וּמִבֵּית עֲבָדִים פְּדִיתִיךָ וָאֶשְׁלַח לְפָנֶיךָ אֶת־מֹשֶׁה אַהֲרֹן וּמִרְיָם׃ ⁵ עַמִּי זְכָר־נָא מַה־יָּעַץ בָּלָק מֶלֶךְ מוֹאָב וּמֶה־עָנָה אֹתוֹ בִּלְעָם בֶּן־בְּעוֹר מִן־הַשִּׁטִּים עַד־הַגִּלְגָּל לְמַעַן דַּעַת צִדְקוֹת יְהוָה׃ ⁶ בַּמָּה אֲקַדֵּם יְהוָה אִכַּף לֵאלֹהֵי מָרוֹם הַאֲקַדְּמֶנּוּ בְעוֹלוֹת בַּעֲגָלִים בְּנֵי שָׁנָה׃ ⁷ הֲיִרְצֶה יְהוָה בְּאַלְפֵי אֵילִים בְּרִבְבוֹת נַחֲלֵי־שָׁמֶן הַאֶתֵּן בְּכוֹרִי פִּשְׁעִי פְּרִי בִטְנִי חַטַּאת נַפְשִׁי׃ ⁸ הִגִּיד לְךָ אָדָם מַה־טּוֹב וּמָה־יְהוָה דּוֹרֵשׁ מִמְּךָ כִּי אִם־עֲשׂוֹת מִשְׁפָּט וְאַהֲבַת חֶסֶד וְהַצְנֵעַ לֶכֶת עִם־אֱלֹהֶיךָ׃ פ ⁹ קוֹל יְהוָה לָעִיר יִקְרָא וְתוּשִׁיָּה יִרְאֶה שְׁמֶךָ שִׁמְעוּ מַטֶּה וּמִי יְעָדָהּ׃ ¹⁰ עוֹד הַאִשׁ בֵּית רָשָׁע אֹצְרוֹת רֶשַׁע וְאֵיפַת רָזוֹן זְעוּמָה׃ ¹¹ הַאֶזְכֶּה בְּמֹאזְנֵי רֶשַׁע וּבְכִיס אַבְנֵי מִרְמָה׃ ¹² אֲשֶׁר עֲשִׁירֶיהָ מָלְאוּ חָמָס וְיֹשְׁבֶיהָ דִּבְּרוּ־שָׁקֶר וּלְשׁוֹנָם רְמִיָּה בְּפִיהֶם׃	Hear now a word: the Lord God has said; Arise, plead with the mountains, and let the hills hear thy voice. ² Hear ye, O mountains, the controversy of the Lord, and *ye* valleys *even* the foundations of the earth: for the Lord *has* a controversy with his people, and will plead with Israel. ³ O my people, what have I done to thee? or wherein have I grieved thee? or wherein have I troubled thee? answer me. ⁴ For I brought tee up out of the land of Egypt, and redeemed thee out of the house of bondage, and sent before thee Moses, and Aaron, and Mariam. ⁵ O my people, remember now, what counsel Balac king of Moab took against thee, and what Balaam the son of Beor answered him, from the reeds to Galgal; that the righteousness of the Lord might be known. ⁶ Wherewithal shall I reach the Lord, *and* lay hold of my God most high? shall I reach him by whole-burnt-offerings, by calves of a year old?

67

with burnt offerings, With yearling calves? ⁷ Does the LORD take delight in thousands of rams, In ten thousand rivers of oil? Shall I present my firstborn *for* my rebellious acts, The fruit of my body for the sin of my soul? ⁸ He has told you, O man, what is good; And what does the LORD require of you But to do justice, to love kindness, And to walk humbly with your God? ⁹ The voice of the LORD will call to the city-- And it is sound wisdom to fear Your name: "Hear, O tribe. Who has appointed its time? ¹⁰ "Is there yet a man in the wicked house, *Along with* treasures of wickedness And a short measure *that is* cursed? ¹¹ "Can I justify wicked scales And a bag of deceptive weights? ¹² "For the rich men of *the* city are full of violence, Her residents speak lies, And their tongue is deceitful in their mouth. ¹³ "So also I will make *you* sick, striking you down, Desolating *you* because of your sins. ¹⁴ "You will eat, but you will not be satisfied, And your vileness will be in your midst. You will *try to*	¹³ וְגַם־אֲנִי הֶחֱלֵיתִי הַכּוֹתֶךָ הַשְׁמֵם עַל־חַטֹּאתֶךָ׃ ¹⁴ אַתָּה תֹאכַל וְלֹא תִשְׂבָּע וְיֶשְׁחֲךָ בְּקִרְבֶּךָ וְתַסֵּג וְלֹא תַפְלִיט וַאֲשֶׁר תְּפַלֵּט לַחֶרֶב אֶתֵּן׃ ¹⁵ אַתָּה תִזְרַע וְלֹא תִקְצוֹר אַתָּה תִדְרֹךְ־זַיִת וְלֹא־תָסוּךְ שֶׁמֶן וְתִירוֹשׁ וְלֹא תִשְׁתֶּה־יָיִן׃ ¹⁶ וְיִשְׁתַּמֵּר חֻקּוֹת עָמְרִי וְכֹל מַעֲשֵׂה בֵית־אַחְאָב וַתֵּלְכוּ בְּמֹעֲצוֹתָם לְמַעַן תִּתִּי אֹתְךָ לְשַׁמָּה וְיֹשְׁבֶיהָ לִשְׁרֵקָה וְחֶרְפַּת עַמִּי תִּשָּׂאוּ׃ פ	⁷ Will the Lord accept thousands of rams, or ten thousands of fat goats? should I give my first-born for ungodliness, the fruit of my body for the sin of my soul? ⁸ Has it *not* been told thee, O man, what *is* good? or what does the Lord require of thee, but to do justice, and love mercy, and be ready to walk with the Lord thy God? ⁹ The Lord's voice shall be proclaimed in the city, and he shall save those that fear his name: hear, O tribe; and who shall order the city? ¹⁰ *Is there* not fire, and the house of the wicked heaping up wicked treasures, and *that* with the pride of unrighteousness? ¹¹ Shall the wicked be justified by the balanced, or deceitful weights in the bag, ¹² whereby they have accumulated their ungodly wealth, and they that dwell in the city have uttered falsehoods, and their tongue has been exalted in their mouth? ¹³ Therefore will I begin to smite thee; I will destroy thee in thy sins. ¹⁴ Thou shalt eat, and shalt not be satisfied; and there shall be darkness upon thee; and he shall depart

remove *for safekeeping*, But you will not preserve *anything*, And what you do preserve I will give to the sword. ¹⁵ "You will sow but you will not reap. You will tread the olive but will not anoint yourself with oil; And the grapes, but you will not drink wine. ¹⁶ "The statutes of Omri And all the works of the house of Ahab are observed; And in their devices you walk. Therefore I will give you up for destruction And your inhabitants for derision, And you will bear the reproach of My people." (Mic. 6:1-16 NAU)		from *thee*, and thou shalt not escape; and all that shall escape shall be delivered over to the sword. ¹⁵ Thou shalt sow, but thou shalt not reap; thou shalt press the olive, but thou shalt not anoint thyself with oil; and *shalt make* wine, but ye shall drink no wine: and the ordinances of my people shall be utterly abolished. ¹⁶ For thou hast kept the statues of Zambri, and *done* all the works of the house of Achaab; and ye have walked in their ways, that I might deliver thee to utter destruction, and those that inhabit the city to hissing: and ye shall bear the reproach of nations.

Process of Discovery
Linguistics Section

Linguistic Structure

> **A** ¹ **Hear now what the LORD is saying**, "Arise, plead your case before the mountains, And let the hills hear your voice. ² "Listen, you mountains, to the indictment of the LORD, And you enduring foundations of the earth, Because the LORD has a case against His people; Even with Israel He will dispute.
>
>> **B** ³ "My people, what have I done to you, **And how have I wearied you?** Answer Me. ⁴ "Indeed, I brought you up from the land of Egypt And ransomed you from the house of slavery, And I sent before you Moses, Aaron and Miriam. ⁵ "My people, remember now What Balak king of Moab counseled And what Balaam son

of Beor answered him, *And* from Shittim to Gilgal, So that you might know the righteous acts of the LORD."

> **B'** ⁶ **With what shall I come to the LORD *And* bow myself before the God on high?** Shall I come to Him with burnt offerings, With yearling calves? ⁷ Does the LORD take delight in thousands of rams, In ten thousand rivers of oil? Shall I present my firstborn *for* my rebellious acts, The fruit of my body for the sin of my soul?

A' ⁸ **He has told you**, O man, what is good; And what does the LORD require of you But to do justice, to love kindness, And to walk humbly with your God?

⁹ The voice of the LORD will call to the city-- And it is sound wisdom to fear Your name: "Hear, O tribe. Who has appointed its time?

A ¹⁰ "Is there yet a man in the wicked house, *Along with* treasures of wickedness And a short measure *that is* cursed? ¹¹ "Can I justify wicked scales And a bag of deceptive weights? ¹² "For the rich men of *the* city are full of violence, Her residents speak lies, And their tongue is deceitful in their mouth.

> **B** ¹³ "So also I will make *you* sick, striking you down, Desolating *you* because of your sins. ¹⁴ "You will eat, but you will not be satisfied, And your vileness will be in your midst. You will *try to* remove *for safekeeping*, But you will not preserve *anything*, And what you do preserve I will give to the sword. ¹⁵ "You will sow but you will not reap. You will tread the olive but will not anoint yourself with oil; And the grapes, but you will not drink wine.

A' ¹⁶ "The statutes of Omri And all the works of the house of Ahab are observed; And in their devices you walk. Therefore I will give you up for destruction And your inhabitants for derision, And you will bear the reproach of My people."

A: Accusation. B: Punishments.[40]

Discussion

This chapter consists of two chiasms. The first chiasm deals with what God requires of us in order to serve Him. The second chiasm refers to the punishment for cheating and violence.

---

[40] "Literary Structure (chiasm, Chiasmus) of Book of Micah." Literary Structure (chiasm, Chiasmus) of Each Pericopes of Book of Micah. Accessed March 14, 2017. http://www.bible.literarystructure.info/bible/33_Micah_pericope_e.html#9. (Literary Structure (chiasm, Chiasmus) of the book of Micah n.d.)

Questioning the Passage

1. What does it mean to plead before the mountains? (v. 1)

    The LORD is telling Israel to raise their voices loudly and publicize the iniquities of the nation, that even the inanimate mountains and hills will hear what is being said. The Targum Yonasan says that the mountains represent the Patriarchs: Abraham, Isaac, and Jacob; and the hills represent the Matriarchs: Sarah, Rebecca, Rachel and Leah. Mahari Kara suggests the mountains represent the kings of the nations of the world and the hills are their officers.[41]

2. What does it mean to let the hills hear your voice? (v. 1)

    This means that the matriarchs will hear the voice of the people crying out to God.

3. What does "listen, you mountains" mean? (v. 2)

    The Sages say that "you mighty ones (mountains), the foundation of the earth," is a reference to the Patriarchs Abraham, Isaac, and Jacob, in whose merit the world exists. God expected Israel to bring the Torah to the world, and that was the foundation of the formation of human happiness.[42]

4. What does the reference to Moses, Aaron, and Miriam mean? (v. 4)

    God sent Moses to teach the Law of God. Aaron was sent to atone for the people's sins. Miriam was sent to instruct the women in the ways of the LORD.[43]

5. What does verse 14 means?

    This is a curse from the LORD because of the wickedness of His people.[44]

---

[41] Scherman, Nosson, Meir Zlotowitz, Sheah Brander, and Menachem Davis. "Micah." In The Prophets: The Later Prophets with a Commentary Anthologized from the Rabbinic Writings. Brooklyn, NY: Mesorah Publications, 2013. p. 275.
[42] IBID. p. 275.
[43] IBID.
[44] IBID. p. 279.

6. What were the statutes of Omri? (v. 16)

    The decrees of Omri and the house of Ahab are references to the golden calves in the Northern Kingdom and the worship of the Baal.[45]

Main/Center Point

The LORD reminds the people through the prophet Micah about how the LORD's love and grace was given freely to Israel. Instead of following the laws and decrees of the LORD, the people in the Northern Kingdom were following the decrees of Omri and Ahab. The decrees of Omri and Ahab were from the pagan rituals of the Baal cult. This angered the LORD to the point of punishing the Northern Kingdom. The Southern Kingdom upon hearing this decree from the LORD unfortunately did not heed the word even though they witnessed the Northern Kingdom's destruction.

People's names

1. מֹשֶׁה *Mosheh* **Meaning:** a great Israel leader, prophet and lawgiver

2. אַהֲרוֹן *Aharon* **Meaning:** an elder brother of Moses

3. מִרְיָם *Miryam* **Meaning:** a sister of Aaron, also a man of Judah

4. בָּלָק *Balaq* **Meaning:** 'devastator,' Moabite king

5. מוֹאָב *Moab* **Meaning:** a son of Lot, also his descendants and the territory where they settled

6. בְּעוֹר *Beor* **Meaning:** 'a burning,' father of an Edomite king, also the father of Balaam

7. עָמְרִי *Omri* **Meaning:** a king of Israel

8. אַחְאָב *Achab* **Meaning:** 'father's brother,' a king of Israel, also a false prophet

---

[45] IBID. p. 281.

Name of places

1. מִצְרָיִם *Mitsrayim* **Meaning:** a son of Ham, also his descendants and their country in N.W.

2. שִׁטִּים *Shittim* **Meaning:** a place E. of the Jordan, also a wadi perhaps West of Jericho

3. גִּלְגָּל *Gilgal* **Meaning:** 'circle (of stones),' the name of several places in Israel

Linguistic Echoes

1. Slavery in the land of Egypt (v. 4)

   This is a reminder to the people about the Passover when God rescued His people from the slavery at the hands of the Egyptians.

2. Balak and Balaam (v. 5)

   Balak and Balaam tried to destroy the nation of Israel. Micah reminds the people of how the LORD showed His love to His people by saving them from destruction.

3. From Shittim (v. 5)

   The daughters of Moab lured the Israelites into immorality and idolatry at Shittim (Numbers chapter 25). Although the entire nation should have been destroyed, only a few sinners died (24,000) in a plague and this atoned for the entire nation, according to Radak.[46]

Thoughts

This message from the LORD is directed toward the sins of the people in the love's light and grace of the LORD. The people are reminded that the LORD kept them from destruction at the hands of Egypt and Moab. The only thing the LORD asked the people to do was to live by the Laws of the LORD. But the people did not. They saw and took part in the rituals of the Baal cult and decided that they liked it. For us today, we remember that

---

[46] IBID.

even though the rituals of a pagan religion might look like fun, they are not sanctioned by the LORD and there will be a punishment if these rituals are followed. Following the LORD may not be glamorous but it is the way to Heaven.

Micah Chapter Seven

Language

New American Standard 1995	Hebrew	Septuagint
¹Woe is me! For I am Like the fruit pickers, like the grape gatherers. There is not a cluster of grapes to eat, Or a first-ripe fig which I crave. ² The godly person has perished from the land, And there is no upright person among men. All of them lie in wait for bloodshed; Each of them hunts the other with a net. ³ Concerning evil, both hands do it well. The prince asks, also the judge, for a bribe, And a great man speaks the desire of his soul; So they weave it together. ⁴ The best of them is like a briar, The most upright like a thorn hedge. The day when you post your watchmen, Your punishment will come. Then their confusion will occur. ⁵ Do not trust in a neighbor; Do not have confidence in a friend. From her who lies in your bosom Guard your lips. ⁶ For son treats father contemptuously, Daughter rises up against her	¹ אַלְלַי לִי כִּי הָיִיתִי כְּאָסְפֵּי־קַיִץ כְּעֹלְלֹת בָּצִיר אֵין־אֶשְׁכּוֹל לֶאֱכוֹל בִּכּוּרָה אִוְּתָה נַפְשִׁי׃ ² אָבַד חָסִיד מִן־הָאָרֶץ וְיָשָׁר בָּאָדָם אָיִן כֻּלָּם לְדָמִים יֶאֱרֹבוּ אִישׁ אֶת־אָחִיהוּ יָצוּדוּ חֵרֶם׃ ³ עַל־הָרַע כַּפַּיִם לְהֵיטִיב הַשַּׂר שֹׁאֵל וְהַשֹּׁפֵט בַּשִּׁלּוּם וְהַגָּדוֹל דֹּבֵר הַוַּת נַפְשׁוֹ הוּא וַיְעַבְּתוּהָ׃ ⁴ טוֹבָם כְּחֵדֶק יָשָׁר מִמְּסוּכָה יוֹם מְצַפֶּיךָ פְּקֻדָּתְךָ בָאָה עַתָּה תִהְיֶה מְבוּכָתָם׃ ⁵ אַל־תַּאֲמִינוּ בְרֵעַ אַל־תִּבְטְחוּ בְּאַלּוּף מִשֹּׁכֶבֶת חֵיקֶךָ שְׁמֹר פִּתְחֵי־פִיךָ׃ ⁶ כִּי־בֵן מְנַבֵּל אָב בַּת קָמָה בְאִמָּהּ כַּלָּה בַּחֲמֹתָהּ אֹיְבֵי אִישׁ אַנְשֵׁי בֵיתוֹ׃ ⁷ וַאֲנִי בַּיהוָה אֲצַפֶּה אוֹחִילָה לֵאלֹהֵי יִשְׁעִי יִשְׁמָעֵנִי אֱלֹהָי׃ ⁸ אַל־תִּשְׂמְחִי אֹיַבְתִּי לִי כִּי נָפַלְתִּי קָמְתִּי כִּי־אֵשֵׁב בַּחֹשֶׁךְ יְהוָה אוֹר לִי׃ ס ⁹ זַעַף יְהוָה אֶשָּׂא כִּי חָטָאתִי לוֹ עַד אֲשֶׁר יָרִיב רִיבִי וְעָשָׂה מִשְׁפָּטִי יוֹצִיאֵנִי לָאוֹר אֶרְאֶה בְּצִדְקָתוֹ׃ ¹⁰ וְתֵרֶא אֹיַבְתִּי וּתְכַסֶּהָ בוּשָׁה הָאֹמְרָה אֵלַי אַיּוֹ יְהוָה אֱלֹהָיִךְ עֵינַי תִּרְאֶינָּה בָּהּ עַתָּה תִּהְיֶה לְמִרְמָס כְּטִיט חוּצוֹת׃ ¹¹ יוֹם לִבְנוֹת גְּדֵרָיִךְ יוֹם הַהוּא יִרְחַק־חֹק׃ ¹² יוֹם הוּא וְעָדֶיךָ יָבוֹא לְמִנִּי אַשּׁוּר וְעָרֵי מָצוֹר וּלְמִנִּי מָצוֹר וְעַד־נָהָר וְיָם מִיָּם וְהַר הָהָר׃ ¹³ וְהָיְתָה הָאָרֶץ לִשְׁמָמָה עַל־יֹשְׁבֶיהָ מִפְּרִי מַעַלְלֵיהֶם׃ ס	¹Alas for me! for I am become as one gathering straw in harvest, and as one gathering grape-gleanings in the vintage, when there is no cluster for me to eat the first-ripe fruit: alas my soul! ² For the godly is perished from the earth; and there is none among men that orders his way aright: they all quarrel even to blood: they grievously afflict every one his neighbour: ³ they prepare their hands for mischief, the prince asks a reward, and the judge speaks flattering words; it is the desire of their soul: ⁴ therefore I will take away their goods as a devouring moth, and as one who acts by a rigid rule in a day of visitation. Woe, woe, thy times of vengeance are come; now shall be their lamentations. ⁵ Trust not in friends, and confide not in guides: beware of thy wife, so as not to commit anything to her. ⁶ For the son dishonours his father, the daughter will rise up against her mother, the daughter-in-law against

mother, Daughter-in-law against her mother-in-law; A man's enemies are the men of his own household.

⁷ But as for me, I will watch expectantly for the LORD; I will wait for the God of my salvation. My God will hear me.

⁸ Do not rejoice over me, O my enemy. Though I fall I will rise; Though I dwell in darkness, the LORD is a light for me.

⁹ I will bear the indignation of the LORD Because I have sinned against Him, Until He pleads my case and executes justice for me. He will bring me out to the light, *And* I will see His righteousness.

¹⁰ Then my enemy will see, And shame will cover her who said to me, "Where is the LORD your God?" My eyes will look on her; At that time she will be trampled down Like mire of the streets.

¹¹ *It will be* a day for building your walls. On that day will your boundary be extended.

¹² It *will be* a day when they will come to you From Assyria and the cities of Egypt, From Egypt even to the Euphrates, Even from sea to sea and mountain to mountain.

¹⁴ רְעֵ֤ה עַמְּךָ֙ בְשִׁבְטֶ֔ךָ צֹ֖אן נַֽחֲלָתֶ֑ךָ שֹׁכְנִ֤י לְבָדָד֙ יַ֔עַר בְּת֖וֹךְ כַּרְמֶ֑ל יִרְע֥וּ בָשָׁ֖ן וְגִלְעָ֖ד כִּימֵ֥י עוֹלָֽם׃

¹⁵ כִּימֵ֥י צֵאתְךָ֖ מֵאֶ֣רֶץ מִצְרָ֑יִם אַרְאֶ֖נּוּ נִפְלָאֽוֹת׃

¹⁶ יִרְא֤וּ גוֹיִם֙ וְיֵבֹ֔שׁוּ מִכֹּ֖ל גְּבֽוּרָתָ֑ם יָשִׂ֤ימוּ יָד֙ עַל־פֶּ֔ה אָזְנֵיהֶ֖ם תֶּחֱרַֽשְׁנָה׃

¹⁷ יְלַחֲכ֤וּ עָפָר֙ כַּנָּחָ֔שׁ כְּזֹחֲלֵ֣י אֶ֔רֶץ יִרְגְּז֖וּ מִמִּסְגְּרֹֽתֵיהֶ֑ם אֶל־יְהוָ֤ה אֱלֹהֵ֙ינוּ֙ יִפְחָ֔דוּ וְיִֽירְא֖וּ מִמֶּֽךָּ׃

¹⁸ מִי־אֵ֣ל כָּמ֗וֹךָ נֹשֵׂ֤א עָוֹן֙ וְעֹבֵ֣ר עַל־פֶּ֔שַׁע לִשְׁאֵרִ֖ית נַחֲלָת֑וֹ לֹא־הֶחֱזִ֤יק לָעַד֙ אַפּ֔וֹ כִּֽי־חָפֵ֥ץ חֶ֖סֶד הֽוּא׃

¹⁹ יָשׁ֣וּב יְרַחֲמֵ֔נוּ יִכְבֹּ֖שׁ עֲוֹנֹתֵ֑ינוּ וְתַשְׁלִ֛יךְ בִּמְצֻל֥וֹת יָ֖ם כָּל־חַטֹּאותָֽם׃

²⁰ תִּתֵּ֤ן אֱמֶת֙ לְיַֽעֲקֹ֔ב חֶ֖סֶד לְאַבְרָהָ֑ם אֲשֶׁר־נִשְׁבַּ֥עְתָּ לַאֲבֹתֵ֖ינוּ מִ֥ימֵי קֶֽדֶם׃

her mother-in-law: those in his house *shall be* all a man's enemies.

⁷ But I will look to the Lord; I will wait upon God my Saviour: my God will hearken to me.

⁸ Rejoice not against me, mine enemy; for I have fallen *yet* shall arise; for though I should sit in darkness, the Lord shall be a light to me.

⁹ I will bear the indignation of the Lord, because I have sinned against him, until he make good my cause: he also shall maintain my right, and shall bring me out to the light, *and* I shall behold his righteousness.

¹⁰ And she that is mine enemy shall see it, and shall clothe herself with shame, who says, Where *is* the Lord thy God? mine eyes shall look upon her: now shall she be for trampling as mire in the ways.

¹¹ *It is* the day of making of brick; that day shall be thine utter destruction, and that day shall utterly abolish thine ordinances.

¹² And thy cities shall be levelled, and parted among the Assyrians; and thy strong cities shall be parted from Tyre to the river, and from sea to sea, and from mountain to mountain.

¹³ And the earth will become desolate because of her inhabitants, On account of the fruit of their deeds. ¹⁴ Shepherd Your people with Your scepter, The flock of Your possession Which dwells by itself in the woodland, In the midst of a fruitful field. Let them feed in Bashan and Gilead As in the days of old. ¹⁵ "As in the days when you came out from the land of Egypt, I will show you miracles." ¹⁶ Nations will see and be ashamed Of all their might. They will put *their* hand on *their* mouth, Their ears will be deaf. ¹⁷ They will lick the dust like a serpent, Like reptiles of the earth. They will come trembling out of their fortresses; To the LORD our God they will come in dread And they will be afraid before You. ¹⁸ Who is a God like You, who pardons iniquity And passes over the rebellious act of the remnant of His possession? He does not retain His anger forever, Because He delights in unchanging love. ¹⁹ He will again have compassion on us; He will tread our iniquities under foot. Yes, You will cast all	¹³ And the land shall be utterly desolate together with them that inhabit it, because of the fruit of their doings. ¹⁴ Tend thy people with thy rod, the sheep of thine inheritance, those that inhabit by themselves the thicket in the midst of Carmel: they shall feed in the land of Basan, and in the land of Galaad, as in the days of old. ¹⁵ And according to the days of thy departure out of Egypt shall ye see marvellous *things*. ¹⁶ The nations shall see and be ashamed; and at all their might they shall lay their hands upon their mouth, their ears shall be deafened. ¹⁷ They shall lick the dust as serpents crawling on the earth, they shall be confounded in their holes; they shall be amazed at the Lord our God, and will be afraid of thee. ¹⁸ Who is a God like thee, cancelling iniquities, and passing over the sins of the remnant of his inheritance? and he has not kept his anger for a testimony, for he delights in mercy. ¹⁹ He will return and have mercy upon us; he will sink our iniquities, and they

their sins Into the depths of the sea. [20] You will give truth to Jacob *And* unchanging love to Abraham, Which You swore to our forefathers From the days of old.		shall be cast into the depth of the sea, *even* all our sins. [20] He shall give blessings truly to Jacob, and mercy to Abraam, as thou swarest to our fathers, according to the former days.

Process of Discovery

Linguistics Section

Linguistic Structure

A ¹ Woe is me! For I am Like the fruit pickers, like the grape gatherers. There is not a cluster of grapes to eat, *Or* a first-ripe fig *which* I crave. ² The godly person has perished from the land, And there is no upright *person* among men. All of them lie in wait for bloodshed; Each of them hunts the other with a net.

  B ³ Concerning evil, both hands do it well. The prince asks, also the judge, for a bribe, And a great man speaks the desire of his soul; So they weave it together. ⁴ The best of them is like a briar, The most upright like a thorn hedge. The day when you post your watchmen, Your punishment will come. Then their confusion will occur.

  B' ⁵ Do not trust in a neighbor; Do not have confidence in a friend. From her who lies in your bosom Guard your lips. ⁶ For son treats father contemptuously, Daughter rises up against her mother, Daughter-in-law against her mother-in-law; A man's enemies are the men of his own household.

A' ⁷ But as for me, I will watch expectantly for the LORD; I will wait for the God of my salvation. My God will hear me. ⁸ Do not rejoice over me, O my enemy. Though I fall I will rise; Though I dwell in darkness, the LORD is a light for me.

A: The believers. B: The evils.

A ⁹ I will bear the indignation of the LORD Because I have sinned against Him, Until He pleads my case and executes justice for me.

  B He will bring me out to the light, *And* I will see His righteousness.

    C ¹⁰ Then my enemy will see, And shame will cover her who said to me, "Where is the LORD your God?" My eyes will look on her; At that time she will be trampled down Like mire of the streets.

  B' ¹¹ *It will be* a day for building your walls. On that day will your boundary be extended. ¹² It *will be* a day when they will come to you From Assyria and the cities of Egypt, From Egypt even to the Euphrates, Even from sea to sea and mountain to mountain.

A' ¹³ And the earth will become desolate because of her inhabitants, On account of the fruit of their deeds.

A: Punishments. B: Salvation. C: Shame of enemies.

A¹⁴ Shepherd Your people with Your scepter, The flock of Your possession Which dwells by itself in the woodland, In the midst of a fruitful field. Let them feed in Bashan and Gilead As in the days of old.

B¹⁵ "As in the days when you came out from the land of Egypt, I will show you miracles." ¹⁶ Nations will see and be ashamed Of all their might. They will put *their* hand on *their* mouth, Their ears will be deaf. ¹⁷ They will lick the dust like a serpent, Like reptiles of the earth. They will come trembling out of their fortresses; To the LORD our God they will come in dread And they will be afraid before You.

B' ¹⁸ Who is a God like You, who pardons iniquity And passes over the rebellious act of the remnant of His possession? He does not retain His anger forever, Because He delights in unchanging love. ¹⁹ He will again have compassion on us; He will tread our iniquities under foot. Yes, You will cast all their sins Into the depths of the sea.

A' ²⁰ You will give truth to Jacob *And* unchanging love to Abraham, Which You swore to our forefathers From the days of old.

A: Wish for salvation. B: Deeds of God.

Discussion

This chapter consists of three chiasms.

Questioning the Passage

1. What is the symbolism of being like fruit pickers? (v. 1)

    The Targum says "like one of the good taken away, in the time when the pious vanished from the land."[47] Micah laments over the pious people who have left Judah and Israel. So many people turned to the Baal worship and other cults that the percentage of pious people decreased.

---

[47] Cathcart, Kevin J., and Martin McNamara. "Chapter 7." In *The Targum of the Minor Prophets*. Collegeville, MN: Liturgical Press, 2005. (K. J. Cathcart 2005)

2. What does it mean "to lie in wait in bloodshed?" (v. 2)

    To wait in bloodshed is an sign that people waited to kill their brothers. Perhaps that wait was because of the cult worship which required human blood to satisfy the false gods.

3. How do people hurt each other with a net? (v. 2)

    "Each one traps the other with the intent to kill, as a hunter traps birds with a net (Radak)."[48]

4. What is the meaning of verse 3?

    Evil benefits when it can bribe judges to rule on their behalf. This was happening during the time of Micah. Justice was not happening. If one had money, one could commit all kinds of crimes and get out of the punishments by bribing judges to rule on their behalf.

5. What is the meaning of "like a briar?" (v. 4)

    The Targum says "It is as difficult for the good among them to get away from his power as from a thorn bush, and for the upright among them as from a thorny edge." "His power" is referring to the power of evil. It is difficult for good people to separate themselves from evil people. It is like being stuck on a briar. One has to get loose from the plant before one can escape. Good people usually become unwanted victims of evil.

6. Is not verse 5 and 6 opposites to the Law to love your neighbor?

    Micah was describing the immorality of his day. A son should exalt his father, but that was not the case. The son would disgrace and humiliate his father in Micah's

---

[48] Scherman, Nosson, Meir Zlotowitz, Sheah Brander, and Menachem Davis. "Micah." In The Prophets: The Later Prophets with a Commentary Anthologized from the Rabbinic Writings. Brooklyn, NY: Mesorah Publications, 2013. p. 281.

day. The same way a daughter rose against her mother to disgrace her. In Micah's day, you could not trust your family, servants or even your slaves (Abarbanel).[49]

7. What is darkness and light? (v. 8)

    Darkness is to be without the love and grace of the LORD. Being in the light is being in presence and love of the LORD.

8. What does "like mire of the streets" mean? (v. 10)

    Mire can be considered mud. People walked through mud as if it was not there if they could not get around it. The children of Israel were like mud on the streets because they were so sinful that the nations surrounding them wanted nothing to do with them.

9. Who will come to whom in verse 12?

    Egypt came from the south and Assyria from the north. The enemies of the LORD will overtake the Promised Land because the LORD has removed His protection from His people because of their sins.

10. What is significance of Bashan and Gilead? (v. 14)

    Bashan and Gilead were fertile pastures on the eastern bank of the Jordan and in ancient times were the home of the tribes of Reuben, Gad and the half tribe Manasseh (Radak, Abarbanel). The days of old are the days of Moses who allocated the different portions of the land to the Tribes of Israel (Metzudos).[50]

---

[49] IBID. p. 283.
[50] IBID. p. 285.

11. What is the significance of "they will put their hand on their mouth?" (v. 16)

    This is what the people will do when they see the miracles of the LORD because they will not be able to speak in the midst of the miracles (Malbim).[51]

12. What is the significance of verse 17?

    "The prophet describes the final humbling of the nations and their awe and reverence for God and Israel (Radak)." The nations will prostate themselves before Israel and it will seem as though they are licking the dust as though they are serpents.[52]

Scripture cross references

Verse 2	Isa 57:1; Isa 59:7; Jer 5:26; Hos 5:1
Verse 3	Pro 4:16, Pro 4:17, Amo 5:12;
Verse 5	Jer 9:4
Verse 6	Mat 10:21, Mat 10:35; Luk 12:53, Mat 10:36
Verse 7	Hab 2:1; Psa 130:5; Isa 25:9; Psa 4:3
Verse 8	Pro 24:17; Oba 1:12; Amo 9:11; Isa 9:2
Verse 12	Isa 19:23-25; Isa 60:4, Isa 60:9
Verse 14	Psa 95:7; Isa 40:11; Isa 49:10; Lev 27:32; Psa 23:4; Jer 50:19; Amo 9:11
Verse 17	Psa 72:9; Isa 49:23; Deu 32:24; Psa 18:45; Isa 25:3; Isa 59:19
Verse 19	Jer 50:20; Isa 38:17; Isa 43:25; Jer 31:34
Verse 20	Gen 24:27; Gen 32:10; Deu 7:8, Deu 7:12

---

[51] IBID. p. 287.
[52] IBID

Main/Center Point

Micah reminds the people of his day that the corruption and total disregard of the LORD's Law will not be tolerated forever. However, the innocent get caught up in the sins of the nations. Therefore, the remnant, those who are loyal to the LORD will be restored to the land. The hope is a remembrance of what the land was like before the corruption. It was a land that flowed with milk and honey and it will again after the sinful people are removed.

Culture Section

Discussion

After the grapes were picked, the vines would be gleaned by the poor. The vineyard would look destitute. The booths established for harvest would come down and the once guarded land would be unguarded. In verse 1, the vineyard is Israel. She was once a mighty country, but in Micah's time she had been reduced to servitude and burden with heavy tributes to foreign powers. Corruption had infiltrated the government and religious practice of the people.[53]

The final words of Micah tell us that the nations of the world would be stunned by the messianic changes that were going to occur. The events surrounding the Messiah where would be so power that people will be taken by surprise. The shamed people of God would rise again. The messianic rule would bring mercy, justice, peace, harmony, and righteousness. The nation of Israel would be restored.[54]

Thoughts

The days of Micah were filled with disrespect of the Laws of God. The people did not care that they were corrupt. Their government had also become corrupt and filled with people

---

[53] Errico, Rocco A., and George M. Lamsa. "Micah Chapter Seven." In Aramaic Light on Ezekiel, Daniel, and the Minor Prophets: A Commentary Based on the Aramaic Language and Ancient Near Eastern Customs. Smyma, GA: Noohra Foundation, 2012.
[54] IBID.

who only cared about themselves and not the well-being of the nation. The LORD stepped in and justice came to the people. However, as with all the prophets, Micah tells us that a remnant of the people will be protected and brought back one day to rebuild the nation. There is an indication that the remnant will be the people who still followed the Laws of the LORD, while everyone around them left the LORD to follow whatever cult beliefs they wanted to.

Bibliography

n.d. *Barefoot Definition and Meaning.* Accessed February 01, 2017. http://www.biblestudytools.com/dictionary/barefoot/.

Version 10. "BibleWorks Software." *Bibleworks for Exegesis and Research.* Norfolk, VA: BibleWorks, LLC.

Bowker, John. 2005. "Isaac Abravanel." In *The Concise Oxford Dictionary of World Religions.* Oxford: England: Oxford University Press.

Bowker, John. 2005. "Isaac Abravanel." In *The Concise Oxford Dictionary of World Religions.* Oxford:England: Oxford University Press.

Cathcart, Kevin J. and R.P. Gordon. 113. *The Targum of the Minor Prophets.* WIlmington, DE: Mesorah Publications.

Cathcart, Kevin J., and Martin McNamara. 2005. *The Targum of the Minor Prophets.* Collegeville, MN: Liturgical Press.

Errico Rocco, George Lamsa. 2012. *Aramaic Light on Ezekiel, Daniel, and the Minor Prophets.* Smyma, GA: Noohra Foundation.

Herman Rosenthal, M. Seligsohn . n.d. *MALBIM, MEÏR LÖB BEN JEHIEL MICHAEL.* Accessed 2 16, 2016. http://www.jewishencyclopedia.com/articles/10325-malbim-meir-lob-ben-jehiel-michael.

n.d. *Jewish Encyclopedia.* Accessed February 14, 2017. JewishEncyclopedia.com.

n.d. *Joseph Kara.* Accessed February 17, 1017. https://www.jewishvirtuallibrary.org/kara-joseph.

n.d. *Literary Structure (chiasm, Chiasmus) of the book of Micah.* Accessed March 14, 2017. http://www.bible.literarystructure.info/bible/33_Micah_pericope_e.html#9.

Mindel, NIssan. n.d. *Rabbi David Kimchi - RaDak.* Brooklyn, NY: Kehot Publication Society.

Scherman, Nosson, Meir Zlotowitz, Sheah Brander, and Menachem Davis. 2013. *The Prophets: The Later Prophets with a Commentary Anthologized the Rabbinic Writings.* Brooklyn:NY: Mesorah Publications.

Sweeney, Marvin Alan, David W Cotter, Chris Frank, and Jerome T. Walsh. 2000. "Micah." In *Micah, Nahum, Habakkuk, Zephanaih, Haggai, Zecharaiah, Malachi,* by Marvin Alan, David W Cotter, Chris Frank, and Jerome T. Walsh Sweeney. Collegeville, MN: Liturgical Press.

n.d. *Targum - Jewish Encyclopedia.* Accessed March 14, 2017. http://www.jewishencyclopedia.com/articles/14248-targum#anchor10.

1948. *THe Univeral Jewish Encyclopedia.* New York: New York: Universal Jewish Encyclopedia.